Moderns – Chaucer to Contemporary Fiction

Moderns – Chaucer to Contemporary Fiction

A. ROBERT LEE

EDINBURGH
University Press

Edinburgh University Press is one of the leading university presses in the UK. We publish academic books and journals in our selected subject areas across the humanities and social sciences, combining cutting-edge scholarship with high editorial and production values to produce academic works of lasting importance. For more information visit our website: edinburghuniversitypress.com

© A. Robert Lee 2025

Edinburgh University Press Ltd
13 Infirmary Street
Edinburgh EH1 1LT

Typeset in 10/12 Adobe Sabon by
IDSUK (DataConnection) Ltd

A CIP record for this book is available from the British Library

ISBN 978 1 3995 4380 4 (hardback)
ISBN 978 1 3995 4382 8 (webready PDF)
ISBN 978 1 3995 4383 5 (epub)

The right of A. Robert Lee to be identified as the author of this work has been asserted in accordance with the Copyright, Designs and Patents Act 1988, and the Copyright and Related Rights Regulations 2003 (SI No. 2498).

Contents

Acknowledgments	vi
Introduction: The Modern	1
1. Medieval Modern: Chaucer and 'Sir Thopas'	10
2. My Lady Mistress: Dame Philology. John Skelton	26
3. Mind's Eye: *Hamlet* and Modernity	39
4. New Made Idiom: John Donne	52
5. A Great Quantity of Heterogeneous Matter: Laurence Sterne	63
6. Era Moderns: Byron, Mary Wollstonecraft Shelley, Peacock	73
7. Like Nobody But Himself: Modern William Hazlitt	84
8. Out of Victorianism: Samuel Butler, Lytton Strachey, Ford Madox Ford	95
9. Cracked Bells and Really Intelligent Detonators: The Modern of Conrad's *The Secret Agent*	107
10. Women's Modern: Mina Loy, Dorothy Richardson, Jean Rhys	123
11. Postmodern Modern: B.S. Johnson, Ann Quin	134
12. Contemporary Modern: Six Fictions	145
Epilogue	157
Index	160

Acknowledgements

To say of *Moderns – Chaucer to Contemporary Fiction* that it has been long aborning borders on serious understatement. On and off it has grown in mind since student years with the added twist that most of my previous literary focus has been on American rather than English literature. So, by birth and first degree, a return to cultural roots as it were.

En route it has had the benefit of discussion with fellow university lifers, most especially in the UK at the University of Kent (1967–96), in Japan, at Nihon University and Waseda University (1997–2011), and in the USA where I also have every cause to be grateful for Visiting academic years at Princeton, the University of Virginia, Bryn Mawr College, Northwestern University, the University of Colorado and the University of California, Berkeley.

Sunderland University, UK, was good enough to make me one of its Annual Visiting Professors for a half-dozen years where I lectured alongside Barry Lewis and Peter Dempsey.

Literary exchanges would have been infinitely poorer without the friendship of late good friends and colleagues. I especially remember debts to Ian Gregor, Mark Kinkead-Weekes, Molly Mahood, R. A. Foakes, Denis Donoghue, Harold Beaver, Tony Tanner, Eric Mottram, John G. Cawelti, Siegfried Mandel and Harrison Hayford.

I need also to give long-standing thanks to Andrew Hook, Gerald Graff, Andrew Gibson, Sanford Marovitz, William H. New, Helmbrecht Breinig, Deborah L. Madsen, Nicholas R. Williams, Cathy Covell Waegner, Ingrid Wendt and David L. Moore.

David Walton in Spain at the University of Murcia gave the book the benefit of encouragement and keenest eye. Douglas Field, likewise, was good enough to read early versions of a number of the book's chapters. Jan Herman helped un-scale some of my prose. Isabel Castelão supplied access to Mina Loy's writings. Lisa Yinwen

ACKNOWLEDGEMENTS

Yu checked a number of bibliographic and page references. Thank you all. Greatly.

I owe a special recognition to Dr Jackie Jones at Edinburgh University Press. She has been wholly generous, and alert, in her support for the book. It has been a bonus to work with her. My appreciation, too, for the work done by the editorial, design and production teams at the press, and especially that of Elizabeth Fraser and Fiona Conn.

As always, debts to Josefa Vivancos Hernández go beyond my deserving.

Introduction:
Modern, Moderns

We can begin with a question. How, exactly, does a literary work assume the mantle of 'modern'? The very etymology of the word, the *modo* and *modernus* of Latin with its meaning of 'just now', might suggest only the current age, a recent yesterday at best. The notion, however, of the one or another kind of modern in connection with English literature in fact possesses a redoubtable legacy. The literal word modern first enters use in the 1500s and through a range of shifts eventually arrives at the culture-movement familiarly installed as modernism. The present account explores, and let it be said for the most part relishes, selective kinds of modern in English literary tradition, whether perceived as such in its own age or taken in retrospect as marker.[1]

This is to draw upon authorship both canonical and otherwise, from established repertoire and from mavericks. Beginning with a faux-epic Chaucer tale, and tracking incrementally down the literary timeline to the metafictions of B. S. Johnson and Ann Quin and beyond, can it be said that modern has ancestry, a linking tradition? Thinking so, to be sure, does not come without risking cavils. Other authors in literature as extensive as medieval to contemporary inevitably exert claims to consideration. Even so, certain writings more evidently than others carry the signage of the bid to engage under deliberately changed terms and conditions.

Wallace Stevens, writing in *Opus Posthumous* (1957), offers an opening benchmark in the observation 'All history is modern history'.[2] In turn Frank Kermode makes a key distinction in *Continuities* (1968):

> Someone should write the history of the word 'modern' . . . That the Modern is a larger and more portentous category than the New our own usage confirms, or at any rate did so until very

2   MODERNS – CHAUCER TO CONTEMPORARY FICTION

lately. The New is to be judged by the criterion of novelty, the Modern implies or at any rate permits a serious relationship with a past, a relationship that requires criticism and indeed radical re-imagining.[3]

G. S. Fraser in *The Modern Writer and His* [sic] *World* points to the phenomenon of the modern with helpful exactness:

> Modern English literature is not a self-contained subject ... when we describe a work as 'modern' we do not merely mean that it has been published (according to the stretch of our historical perspective) in the past five or ten years, in the past fifty or sixty years, or perhaps since the Renaissance. When we describe a work as 'modern' we are ascribing, however vaguely, certain intrinsic qualities to it. We find something 'modern' in Catullus, but not in Virgil; in Villon, but not in Ronsard; in Donne, but not in Spenser; in Clough, but not in Tennyson. There is something in the mood of each of these three pairs of writers – something abrupt, restless, mocking, dissatisfied, possibly – that comes home to us today in a way in which the more serene and elaborate art of their partners, here, does not.[4]

Abruptness, restlessness, mockery, clearly play their part. Another 'intrinsic quality' does so equally, the willingness to step outside, even subvert, customarily expected guardrails of genre or language.[5] On occasion that has meant the recognisable avant-garde. On others it remains less explicit, the 'mood' Fraser seizes upon, oblique but canny self-awareness of new deportment.

In the advent of modernism, English, British, American, European or more globally, and of the postmodern, the stance turns explicit – Pound's rousing mantra of Make it New. Which, emphatically, is not to say that *Moderns – Chaucer to Contemporary Fiction* argues for writings whose modernity offers mere prologue, or for that matter the aftermath, to modernism. Kermode's distinction between new and modern sharply applies. Rather, from the medieval age onwards, these are forms of the literary modern within the longer timeline with rights to their own styles of making. Modernism or the postmodern, in consequence, signify literary-cultural iterations of the modern, innovative, select, but existent within always evolving literary history.

INTRODUCTION 3

The idea of the modern in English, as in other literature, has had a well enough known variety of manifestations. The Middle Ages found Latin under contestation from emergent early modern English. The Renaissance into the eighteenth century saw the battle of Ancients and Moderns, the classical as against the vernacular. The Romantic era pitched for new sensibility, feeling, vision, over literary rules and decorum. It was as modernity that reaction set in against Victorianism. The very use of a term like postmodern attests to move-along, the sense of changing prospect.[6]

It so bears re-emphasis that *Moderns* argues for no totalising paradigm. The writers at issue, again down literary time, possess their discrete qualities in mode of narration, challenge to genre. To this end I have tried to keep a careful margin of distinction between them and the Anglo-American literary modernists most associated with Henry James, T. S. Eliot or Virginia Woolf, and with Joyce, always, as pioneering helmsman. It is in this regard that chapter terms, starting with 'medieval modern' and arriving at 'contemporary moderns', come into play.

What, then, is the rationale behind examining this 'modern' trajectory? Both Kermode and Fraser, respectively, give pointers. The modern possesses its own history whose literary expression 'comes home to us today'. That involves giving heed to the discernible ways these writings specifically determine upon new terms of engagement with their readers, or put otherwise, the effort to making them feel contemporary with the author. The selection of names taken up in this account in this respect especially challenge time-barriers or genre, each the bearer of their own flag.

We meet Chaucer in the late fourteenth century only to encounter an example of his writing that exhibits a flourish of contemporary-seeming ventriloquy. *Hamlet* belongs to the Elizabethan stage yet lives on in our own interior soliloquies. Laurence Sterne inhabits Augustan England even as he steps from inside his own text to speak as though today's narrative confidant. You read Hazlitt and for the moment imagine his columns to be fresh reportage. Conrad turns 'realism' about face, a key novel that makes one kind of 'history' the masquerade of another. Samuel Butler, late Victorian, teases to intriguing good purpose the very notion of autobiography just as Lytton Strachey does so for 'standard' biography. Why, in reading Mina Loy or Dorothy Richardson or Jean Rhys, as much as in reading an established modernist like Ford Madox Ford, do we think them quite readily of our own time, eye and pitch? Subsequent tiers, whether B. S. Johnson or Ann Quin who steer the modern towards postmodern, or a choice of contemporary novelists each of whom adds a different modern, offer a change of light to the trajectory at large. This is not step-for-step continuity, as the chapters on Skelton and Byron and contemporaries bear witness, but more to be thought a gallery of exhibits.

Nor does this account seek to detach the chosen authorship from historical and technological contexts. The printing press, advances in science from cosmology to circulation of blood to evolution, help shape how the modern comes to be perceived. Technology, likewise, gives its markers, whether microscope, map or new globes in earlier times, computer, pdf or audio book in those to follow. Bookselling and the rise of a reading public, together with the literary review, share changing space with graphic novel or screen-time at the internet, app and ebook. These matrices, to which I return in the Epilogue, in no way are to be overlooked but the emphasis even so always comes back to the modernity of imagination within the writings themselves: or so insists the argument at hand.

I am perfectly aware that *Moderns* travels a wide concourse and assumes a willingness to read, or have read, energetically in English literature. Even so, I hope the debutant reader with, say, a Shakespeare play, an early novel (whether or not in popular culture form like *Frankenstein*), or a later century's bestseller like *Girl, Woman, Other* in their repertoire, will find a stimulus to thinking how literature indeed speaks from beyond its historical footholds. More seasoned readers, themselves once debutant like myself, I also hope will find a pattern of fresh approach.

In taking on breadth, as well as specificity, *Moderns* aims to show 'the modern' as actually, and paradoxically, long-standing, and to repeat, in effect different rungs down an extending ladder. Other authorship, to again offer acknowledgement, plausibly could be brought to bear. The writings addressed occupy discrete ground, not to be extricated from context but at the same time singularities. It remains only to move into their congenial particularity for confirmation.

Unlikely as may be, how first to speak of the poetry of Chaucer in connection with the modern? Does he not carry the very banner of the

INTRODUCTION 5

English Middle Ages? Yet for all that the verse-stories in *The Canterbury Tales* could not seem more rooted in his age, one in particular has about it defiance, quite the oddity. The issue gathers of what, exactly, Chaucer, or 'Chaucer' as persona, is up to in contributing his 'Tale of Thopas' and follow-through with 'The Tale of Melibee'. The Host's judgement that 'Thy drasty ryming is nat worth a toord!' ranks among the most wonderfully summary, and obviously excremental, of all literary dismissals. Chaucer, or his persona, allows himself to be purposely demeaned. After all he tells a tale that teases the very errantry it purports to celebrate, and then, in the homiletic 'Melibee', has that parochially be misread by the Host as supplying a gloss for his domestic marital relationship. The argument explores the ways the conscious pastiche at play in 'Sir Thopas', and its link to the voicing of the Prologue, conveys the modern in Chaucer to perfection.

How, in similar vein, to take measure of John Skelton? It has become commonplace to see him as the bridge figure, late medieval to early Renaissance. Equally, he contends as a voice speaking as though the contemporary literary duellist, at once learned yet readily vernacular in turn of expression. Re-reading his better-known verse, 'Phyllyp Sparow', 'Colyn Cloute', 'Why Come Ye Nat to Courte', and above all and despite its occasional obliquity 'Speke, Parrot', there can be no hiding the suspicion that the poet almost patently wants to throw his poetics in the reader-listener's face, precisely the 'ragged, tattered and jagged' rhyme as he calls it in 'Colyn Cloute'. To which end the poem also speaks of being 'rudely rayne beaten', as though the upshot of being summoned from within the poet's internal stormy weather. The collage, and the sonics, with 'Speke, Parrot' the crest of his verse, lay plausible grounds for arguing how Skelton attests to the modern.

Hamlet. Hamletism. Which of Shakespeare's plays more seeks to take cognisance of Being? To be or not to be indeed. *Dasein.* This is Shakespeare taken up with ontology, *Hamlet* as embodying, or in a self-reflecting sense, acting out philosophical speculation in kind with Montaigne's 'Que sais-je?'. Hamlet's soliloquies, the play within a play, the screens between seeming and actual, double-vision and double-perception, death as either life's tragedy or Yorick's graveyard joke, build into the holding pattern. Revenge-tragedy as category limits the play, its supreme inquisition into borders of being and non-being. Hamlet's querying anticipates modern phenomenological struggle, or as Wittgenstein would confirm, language itself in

6   MODERNS – CHAUCER TO CONTEMPORARY FICTION

the very making of self and world. The modern, as written in *Hamlet*, affords few more compelling anatomies.

In John Donne English Renaissance poetry has its modern standard-bearer. Schooled in the classics, church doctrine, even warfare, he speaks as though ever the contemporary, the custodian of rare audacity be it earthly love or godly belief. His wit and paradox have been infinitely noted, whether Dr Johnson's celebrated misgiving as to 'heterogeneous ideas . . . yoked by violence together' ('Cowley'), H. T. C. Grierson's early twentieth-century case for recovery of his writing, or T. S. Eliot's praise of 'unification of sensibility'.[7] The phrase 'new made idiom' appears in 'A Valediction: of the Booke', a paean to love as itself the album of life engaged at once in bodily flesh and ethereality of spirit. It has about it the perfect Donne stamp, text as life, life as text, the one vividly entwined in the other. Poem after poem exhibits the confidence, the ingenuity, to carry the footfalls of its making right into the very life-matter it seeks to dramatise. That, as much as ostensible sexual or theological ardour, plays a major part in why Donne's modernity goes on summoning enthusiasm.

From the playful tease of unwound clock and the disturbed conception of Tristram as *homunculus* through to 'the best of its kind' cock and bull story as it is finally judged by Yorick, the nine volumes of Laurence Sterne's *Tristram Shandy* could not better give meaning to the notion of performative text. The digressive energies, the sequences in Latin, even the print-forms of asterisks and extravagant hyphenations, might be Paul Klee's lines out for a walk. Is not, too, the novel given over to its very materiality as physical 'book'? Tristram Shandy's 'life and opinions' continues to stir dissent. Want of purpose, lack of coherence, run the charges. But the more approving view argues for Sterne's novel as banner, and let it be said modern, imaginative figuration of mind.

To move into the modern of the arriving early nineteenth century invites the perhaps less than usual route. Poetry, to be sure, had been directed to new vision, renewed mythology, in the visionary work of Blake and in the *Lyrical Ballads*. Fiction under the pen of Jane Austen, and from *Sense and Sensibility* onwards, had given advance to the ironies of courtship, domesticity, gender. But in Lord Byron, Mary Wollstonecraft Shelley and Thomas Love Peacock, change of temperament becomes irrefutable. 'Childe Harold' and 'Don Juan' play their parts in the formation of The Byronic while investing the Spenserian stanza with a recognisable

INTRODUCTION 7

turn of virtuosity. *Frankenstein; or, The New Prometheus*, vintage horror by repute, conceals far more encompassing philosophical parable. *Nightmare Abbey*, comic ventriloquism and mock Gothic, takes 'modern' shy at not just the postures of English Romanticism but literary posturing in the round.

Hazlitt as practitioner of both the literary and the familiar essay advances discursive writing from Addison and Steele and the columns of their bestselling *Spectator Magazine* into the restyled modern. His groundbreaking is to be met in *Characters of Shakespear's Plays* (1817) and *Lectures on the English Poets* (1818) and the rounds of observation of *Table Talk* (1821) and *The Spirit of the Age* (1825). His commentaries assign fresh critical particularisation both to Shakespeare and the Romantics and to the vernacular life he takes up in 'The Fight' or 'The Indian Jugglers'. His eulogy to Montaigne suggests a working reflection, both of them cynosures in shaping the essay-form.

Whatever reputation Samuel Butler's *The Way of All Flesh* (1873–84, published 1903) maintains, a hail and farewell to Victorian values, an early psychoanalytical as much as autobiographical life-and-times account, it also functions as a work of *Pensées*. Modern subjects hold throughout, childhood and family, schooling, socialisation, and the general liberation of self. Butler earns his stripes in the use of Ernest Pontifex as his other self and, in his narrator, as his *alter vox*. Lytton Strachey writes *Eminent Victorians* (1918), the de-idealising portraiture of an age's celebrity quartet, from a later, and savvier, vantage-point. His carefully tempered stealth sets new interpretative standards for biography. Ford Madox Ford's *The Good Soldier* (1915) escalates into modernism, the new-century society inherited from Victorianism caught short. Gentility masks bad faith. Marriage betrays. Narration in the novel works to purpose, true or false storyteller, modern/modernist indeterminacy of viewpoint.

To invoke the Joseph Conrad of *The Secret Agent* (1907) is first to contest any categorisation of standard spy-thriller. For the novel dissimulates brilliantly, about-face detection. The storyline of bombing the Greenwich Observatory guys neo-realism, whether the explosion or the conspiracy behind it. Conrad creates masquerade, the mimicry beyond true-to-life surface. The anarchists, the state figures from government ministers to the Scotland Yard police who pursue them, Verloc and Winnie, even Stevie, resemble actors

8   MODERNS – CHAUCER TO CONTEMPORARY FICTION

caught up in a political script as virtual as actual. London, as locale, correspondingly takes its place as real-unreal city. Conrad so creates the one version always the 'modern' refraction of the other.

The literary modernist, under feminist colours, possesses its best-known avatar in Virginia Woolf, the novels and essays. But it has bordered on negligence to underplay accompanying and ongoing generational lineage. In Mina Loy, futurist poet, watercolourist, oil painter, sculptor and assembly-artist and designer, one kind of women's modern declares itself. In Dorothy Richardson, whose thirteen-volume Pilgrimage series (1915–67) charts the awakening life of her protagonist Miriam Henderson, there stands another. Jean Rhys takes on subsequent modern standing through *Wide Sargasso Sea* (1966), intertext with *Jane Eyre*, multi-inflected, postcolonial, and written four decades on from the bow she made with *The Left Bank and Other Stories* (1927).

Postmodern moderns? The phrasing represents an effort to meet the originality of a 1960s–70s pairing like B. S. Johnson and Ann Quin through two highlighted works by each. In *The Unfortunates* (1969), with its novel-in-a-box format, and *House Mother Normal: A Geriatric Comedy* (1970), dark, antic soliloquies given over to life's edge, Johnson shows his narrative chance. Ann Quin's novels, likewise, stand out against the fiction of her time. *Berg* (1964) transposes the seaside tranquillity of England's Brighton into a macabre alternative-world of psychosis and sexuality. *Three* (1966), much influenced by the French New Novel, operates on the joining and slippages of memory, and in triangulated storytelling that denies not only closed ending but, wryly, closed beginning and middle.

Contemporary moderns, the ultimate chapter, explores largely city-centred novels in which English history and its cultural formation, be it ethnicity or sexuality, comes under widening regard.[8] This enlargement of compass has equally made for new visibilities of narrative regime, not unexpectedly given three Booker prizewinning performances. Six names feature, those of Bernardine Evaristo, Kamila Shamsie, Diran Adebayo, Xiaolu Guo, Howard Jacobson and Alan Hollinghurst. The Epilogue briefly ponders the implications of the writings explored, a continuum, perhaps more exactly a variorum: medieval to Elizabethan, Augustan to Victorian, Modernist to Postmodern.

Modern, it will not be doubted, requires a degree of elasticity in the way it is deployed in the present study. It does not assume

INTRODUCTION 9

the fixed template, the one presiding definition. In creating their own individual species of modern, the writers at the centre of each chapter might indeed best be thought a gallery, at once self-distinguishing but linked overall in temperament. They make us more than usual co-makers in taking hold of the writing they bequeath.

Notes

1. I am conscious that the appropriative use of English as against, say, British raises issues. Another volume could be written on literary moderns in Irish (Laurence Sterne, though born in Ireland, never lived there), Scottish and Welsh literatures. Nor do I assume English as register covers other Anglophone literatures, whether Atlantic or Pacific, African or Asian.

2. Wallace Stevens, *Opus Posthumous: Poems, Plays, Prose*, New York: Vintage Books, Adagio Notebooks, 1957. Re-issued edn. Milton J. Bates, New York: Knopf Doubleday, 1990.

3. Frank Kermode, 'Modernisms', *Continuities*, London: Routledge & Kegan Paul, 1968, 27.

4. G. S. Fraser, *The Modern Writer and His World*, Harmondsworth, Middlesex: Penguin Books/Pelican, 1964, 12.

5. In this respect I have benefited from Winifred Nowottny, *The Language Poets Use*, London: The Athlone Press, 1962. I also pay due to her as one of my early university teachers.

6. The modern, to be sure, has come under transnational and theoretical auspices, though mainly with a view to the emergence of modernism. See, notably, Paul de Man, 'Literary History and Literary Modernity', *Daedalus*, 99:12, 384–404, Spring 1970, and 'What is Modern?', review of Richard Ellman and Charles Feidelson (eds), *The Modern Tradition: Backgrounds of Modern Literature*, *The New York Review*, 26 August 1976.

7. Samuel Johnson, 'Cowley', *The Lives of the Poets*, re-issued, Oxford and New York: Oxford Oxford University Press, 2006; H. J. C. Grierson, *The Poems of John Donne*, 2 vols, Oxford: Oxford University Press, 1912, and *Metaphysical Lyrics and Poems of the Seventeenth-Century: Donne to Butler*, Oxford: Clarendon Press, 1921; and T. S. Eliot, review of *Metaphysical Lyrics and Poems of the Seventeenth Century: Donne to Butler*, *Times Literary Supplement*, 20 October 1921.

8. Some three decades ago I made an attempt to meet these developments. See A. Robert Lee (ed.), *Other Britain, Other British: Contemporary Multicultural Fiction*, London: Pluto Press, 1995.

CHAPTER I

Medieval Modern: Chaucer and 'Sir Thopas'

Wherefore I biseke yow mekely, for the mercy of God, that ye preye for me that Crist have mercy on me and foryeve me my giltes; and namely of my translacions and enditynges of worldly vanitees, the whiche I revoke in my retracciouns: as is the book of Troilus; the book also of Fame; the book of the XXV. Ladies; the book of the Duchesse; the book of Seint Valentynes Day of the Parlement of Briddes; the tales of Caunterbury, thilke that sownen into synne . . . and many a song and many a leccherous lay; that Crist for his grete mercy foryeve me the synne. But of the translacion of Boece de Consolacione, and othere bookes of legendes of seintes, and omelies, and moralitee, and devocioun that I thanke oure Lord Jhesu Crist and his blissful Mooder, and alle the seintes of hevene . . .

Geoffrey Chaucer, 'Heere taketh the makere
of this book his leve'[1]

How to read this leave-taking at the close of Chaucer's career? Does it truly represent 'retraccions' of his writing's different turns to worldly issues? It may indeed be that he does believe 'giltes' should attach to the *Book of Troilus*, *The House of Fame*, *The Book of the Duchess*, and the twenty-four narratives that make up his *Tale of Caunterbury*. There may be sincerity in his misgivings at 'many a song and many a leccherous lay' and any tendency to have fallen short of the virtues his 'litel tretys' designates 'moralitee', 'devocioun' and 'grace'. We are also enjoined to believe that his soul will fare the better if he is remembered as the translator of *Boece* (despite Boethius's neo-Platonism in *Consolations of Philosophy*) and of 'othere bookes of legends, seintes, and omelies'. Suspicions, however, press and hover.

10

Not a few flintier-eyed readers have had their doubts that Chaucer's 'tranlacions and enditynges of the worldly vanitees' truly do deserve retraction on grounds of 'myn unkonnyngee' or that he would 'have seyd better if I had konnynge'? To include 'the tales of Caunterbury' especially would mean denial of the worldliness that inspires much of his best imagining, the confirming touch of quotidian life. Is this truly 'meke' supplication or an author slyly, knowingly, and can we say *modernly*, covering his tracks?

Nowhere better than in *The Canterbury Tales* does Chaucer personalise his writing in ways that animate, and exceed, customary attributions of medieval world view. In the case of 'The Prologue and Tale of Sir Thopas', odd man out if ever there were in the *Tales*, the voice speaks tactically from both outside and inside and as conscious a piece of staging as any in his oeuvre. Chaucer enters his own text as 'Chaucer' the apparently affectless, not to say portly, figure among the Prologue's 'nyne and twenty in a compaignye/ of sondry folk'. Harry Bailey, gamesome host of the Tabard Inn in Southwark, identifies him as holder-back, 'a popet', eyes dozily upon the ground. Called upon for his story, the metrical fandango of a romance 'Chaucer' takes upon himself to unfold, with its gallop and excess of adjective, provokes one of the most celebrated put-downs in literary history – the Host's infamous 'Thy drasty ryming is not worth a toord!'.

A double-fold is involved. Chivalry falls under mock-styling in 'Sir Thopas'. The ensuing prose homily, delivered *au grand sérieux* in the form of 'The Tale of Melibee', makes the perfect contrast. The two tales, 'the best rym I kan' and 'moral tale virtuous', pair together in wonderfully attractive discord. They mirror, and at the same time highlight, Chaucer's subtly insinuated presence in the *Tales* overall, insider narrative savvy that gives due pointers to his particular kind of reflexive 'modern' virtuosity.

This is to suggest a Chaucer fully willing to acknowledge, and in the case of 'Sir Thopas' to satirise, the very textuality he is putting on offer. He so invites recognition of story-making as itself story in the pilgrimage. Can it altogether surprise that a latter-day photographer like Diane Arbus, renowned for her craftily composed images, looks back through the centuries to Chaucer as inspiration? Would not this be one modern referencing another modern, the click of camera as against the meticulousness of quill?

MODERNS – CHAUCER TO CONTEMPORARY FICTION

A first marker is that 'The Tale of Thopas' follows 'The Prioress's Tale' with its vengeful story of the supposed Jewish conspiratorial blood murder of the Christian child who continues to sing after death. Albeit set in an Asian ghetto, it re-tells the hoary myths of Jewish betrayal, and murder, of Jesus Christ, and the memory of 'cursed Jewes' in the story of Hugh of Lincoln. The reaction of the Canterbury-bound pilgrim company is duly contemplative:

> Whan seyd was al this miracle, every man
> As sobre was that wonder was to se.
> (Prologue to Sir Thopas)

It takes the Host to lighten the mood ('oure Hooste japen tho began').

He alights upon the 'Chaucer' whom he enjoins to 'looke up murily', act true to the Falstaffian implication of his waistline, speak out from behind his 'elvyssh' countenance, and break free from any withholding of 'daliaunce'. This 'Chaucer' is to deliver nothing short of 'som deyntee thing'. In the event, the Host and his fellow travellers will get perversely other than what they bargain for, a tale in which 'daintiness' and 'myrth' are themselves guyed, whose energies lie in pastiche. Were that not enough, 'Melibee' as replacement story will turn on the opposite axis, high sententiousness, moral parable.

The two fits or cantos of 'Sir Thopas', the one given in full, the second a fragment in consequence of the Host's intervention, begin with a storyteller's bond ('I wol telle verrayment'). Ahead lies less true verity than true lie, although buttressed with the promise of 'myrthe' and 'solas', the latter in its meaning of entertainment. Knighthood stands centre-frame, though knighthood enclosed in language that deflates even as it eulogises in the uses of 'fair' and 'gent' (here genteel) and heady invocations of 'bataille' and 'tourneyment'. The title-figure ('his name was sire Thopas') is brought forth as a 'doghty swayn'. Chaucer has him enter as though deserving of courtly announcement, gemstone subsumed into his very name (topaz) to befit his rank. The ironies are so in place. The promised metrical romance resembles adult nursery story, skewed genre. Modern Chaucer is so launched.[2]

Chaucer clearly relishes the challenge of putting his pastiche to work. Sir Thopas, of 'fer contree', is Flemish, from the ancestral trading city of Poperinghe rather than France, and so, to onlookers, would have been of chivalry's second order. Physiology edges

CHAUCER AND 'SIR THOPAS'

towards misproportion. In face he is likened to white-flour bread ('payndemayn') with rose-red lips. His general complexion favours scarlet. Long saffron hair trails down his back. Most, he displays a distinguished proboscis ('he hadde a seemly nose'). Thopas is to be thought the excessively peerless deer hunter, horseman, archer, river hawker albeit of lesser species of hawk ('grey goshawk on honde'). Were these qualities not sufficient, he fulfils a maiden's dream of paramour, himself as chaste as Nature's bramble-flowers bearing red berries. Cartoon errantry prevails.

Sartorial excess likewise comes into view. Thopas vaunts his 'fyn and cleere' vesture, breeches, shirt, protective mail tunic, Jewish-manufactured plate hauberk with its lily-flower coats of arms, and shield emblazoned with jokey boar's head and carbuncle. Deluxe Spanish leather shoes clad his feet. He has showy brown hose from Bruges and a costly robe. Other accoutrements include copper helmet, whalebone saddle, shining bridle, cypress-wood lance and dappled horse. This ostentation, Sir Thopas as clothes-horse, equally works as verbal self-clothing, deliberate showpiece. Chaucer's confected story, sworn to by Thopas 'on ale and breed', requires wholly-to-purpose confected language.

The modern guying persists. Nature transposes into fantasy arcadia, the opposite of Spenser's later bower of bliss. Thopas rides through forests of 'bukke and hare', male and female game, less elevated hunting than, say, deer or boar. He spurs his grey steed, lance in hand, long sword by his side, as though the model of chivalric demeanour. The forest positively abounds in rising sap. Grass springs forth. Ginger, liquorice and clove give off perfume. Sparrowhawk, popinjay (or parrot), throstlecock and turtle-dove provide less avian chorus than burlesque.

Thopas is said to conjure in dream an elf-queen as 'lemman' (lover) and to launch forth upon knightly quest into a 'prive woon' (dwelling-place), secret terrain. There he will have his jousting ground with 'sire Olifaunt' (Sir Elephant), the ogre prison-keeper of 'the queene of Fayerye' who reigns with 'harpe and pipe and symphonye'. The giant's threat ('Anon I sle thy steed/ With mace') and Thopas's riposte ('Tomorwe wol I meet with thee,/ Whan I have myn armoure') give figuration to dark against light. To add impetus before the pending joust he finds himself obliged to flee the stones flung his way, a reversal of David and Goliath. Battle, or rather mock-battle, remains to be joined, the parody of arms and the man.

MODERNS – CHAUCER TO CONTEMPORARY FICTION

In furtherance 'Chaucer' shows no compunction at intruding into his tale, the modern artificer. His show of bonhomie appears as unlimited as his self-applause ('Yet listeth, lordes, to my tale/ Murier than the nightyngale'). He almost willingly concedes that the knight ('with sydes smale') and giant ('with hevedes three') loom as figures keyed to make-believe. In signalling charade the tale offers itself as double-dealing to a fault, the very fantasy of a fantasy. From the outset, and throughout 'Sir Thopas', the Chaucer behind 'Chaucer' implicitly revels in the artifice, the tale's sleight of hand.

Sir Thopas's rallying cry for 'jolitee', 'game and glee', on the eve of battle, is added to in 'gestours for to tellen tales of romances'. These will be stories to give support to his own heady fabling of royalty, popes, cardinals and lover-pairs. The prospect of culinary luxury does shared duty, a feast-ahead of 'sweet wyn', 'mede', 'roial spicerie', 'gyngebreed', 'lycorys', and as though a special treat, 'sugre that is trye'. Chaucer as 'Chaucer' makes the one plenitude mimic the other, comestibles for word.

As he moves towards closing the First Fit, Chaucer has his persona speak to the pilgrim listeners as though, audaciously, he and they share bonds of story:

> Loo, lordes myne, here is a fit!
> If ye wol any of it,
> To tell it wol I fonde.

Exhilarated, keen to hold his audience, with a request for pause in any conversation being conducted by his listeners, he adopts the privileges of modern author:

> Now holde youre mouth, *par charitee*
> Bothe knight and lady free,
> And herkneth to my spelle;
> Of bataille and chivalry
> And of ladyes love-drury
> Anon I wel yow telle.

The peremptory commands to 'holde youre mouth' and 'herkneth to my spelle' flaunts willingness to cause irritation. The promise of endless story given over to 'bataille' and 'love-drury' (passionate love) has become meta-story, 'Chaucer' at the behest of Chaucer again displayed inside the self-same story he is telling.

To have the story place Sir Thopas in the romance genealogy of Sir Horn, Sir Hypotis, Sir Bevis, Sir Guy and others is to see in him another image of an image. How not so as the hero astride horse with lily-flowered coat of arms on full display? As 'auntrous' (adventurous) knight, he is said to sleep not in house nor palace but upon Nature's earth, hood for a blanket, helmet for a pillow, his water drawn pure from the well. The comparison with 'sire Percyvell', authentic 'worthy', makes for a final deflationary slap.

It is the prospect of breathless surfeit ('Til on a day – . . .') that prompts the Host, likely to the relief of listeners both inside and outside the text, to cry 'Namoore of this, for Goddes dignitee'. The response caustically shows bluff comic impatience, tired ear. It works equally to advance Chaucer's satire of himself, of Thopas as delegate teller, and of the curtailed tale being told. The story of 'Sir Thopas' pivots and circles back on its own telling, the medieval stamp of the modern.

The arising colloquy between 'Chaucer' and Host, at once coda to 'The Tale of Sir Thopas' and preface to 'The Tale of Melibee', makes for a next round of reflexive fashioning. First comes the Host's intervention, his 'Myn eres aken of thy drasty speche' and un-appealable dismissal of 'swich a rym' as 'rym doggerel'. The summing-up, brute, succinct, Anglo-Saxon, understandably has become legend, the 'drasty ryming' deserving only excrementally worded short shrift. The plaintive response of 'Chaucer', would-be equal opportunity storyteller, matches in his hope of continuing.

> . . . why wiltow lette me
> Moore of my tale than another man
> Syn that it is the beste rym I kan?

The implication that this is actually the worst kind of 'beste rym I kan' hints of Chaucer's relish at rounding on his narrative sharer, and on acknowledging the carefully inlaid text.

In obliging 'Chaucer' to requisition a new tale, the Host tacitly acts for Chaucer himself. The reciter of 'Sir Thopas' is not to 'dependeth' (waste) time, and to entertain yet at the same time exhibit 'som doctrine'. 'Gladly' is the response, ironic affability in a storyteller whose immediate previous flow has been cut off mid-stream. The tale he proposes, that of 'Melibee', which he says he has told many times

16   MODERNS – CHAUCER TO CONTEMPORARY FICTION

(thus contradicting the assertion made at the outset of 'Sir Thopas' that 'For oother tale certes kan I noone'), will be 'moral', 'virtuous', duly pledged to gravitas. He also, one has to assume in accord with Chaucer's own sense of storytelling, allows that successive tellings or recitations spontaneously change even as they renew the original. The implication might be that no canon ever remains free of adjustment, a familiar enough modern assumption.

The invocation of Matthew, Mark, Luke and John in connection with the tale 'Chaucer' next proposes again carries double implication. There can be no whole gospel truth in storytelling even in the matter of 'the peyne of Jhesu Crist'. Rather in 'hir tellyng difference' we are to recognise the competition of different versions, even if, in sum, 'nathelees hir sentence is al oon'. This formulation of the one tale folded into different tellings exactly looks back to 'Sir Thopas' and forward to 'The Tale of Melibee'. They not only counter one another in subject but in verse metre as against homiletic prose. In this regard Chaucer, as 'Chaucer', insists upon making another apology:

> And though I nat the same wordes saye
> As ye han herd, yet to yow alle I preye
> Blameth me nat . . .

The entreaty to be excused for giving new style to old fare ('nat the same wordes'), be it to then-and-there listeners or to any eventual reader of the *Tales*, could not be more agreeably disingenuous.

'The Tale of Melibee', precisely because familiar through re-tellings, Chaucer affirms can have no canonical version. The one telling subsumes the other. Before 'Melibee', however, Chaucer has 'Chaucer' try one last request to continue on with 'Sir Thopas' ('lat me tellen al my tale, I preye'). The action of Chaucer using 'Chaucer' to solicit indulgence for the predications of his own style ('If that yow thynke I varie as in my speche') amounts to serious play of author and mask. The would-be continuance of high romance, or at least in the satiric version of it given by 'Chaucer', is to be reminded of Chaucer in full medieval-modern ironic mode.

'Sir Thopas' presents itself as deliberate fragment, or at least is made to appear so having been editorially severed by the Host. Its ostensible begetter, 'Chaucer', is wrong-footed, and yet not, told to pack his bags as one kind of storyteller, and yet given the chance to redeem himself in another. In these respects the one tale, and the manner of its telling, throws light upon Chaucer's larger authorial strategy in *The Canterbury Tales*. For none of the tales come without their author's custodial signalling. Chaucer in fact rarely fails to give notice as self-acknowledging authorial presence, whether as the narrator of General Prologue, the 'Chaucer' of 'Sir Thopas', the valedictorian of the brief 'Lenvoy de Chaucer' after 'The Clerk's Tale', or the Host as intervening master of ceremonies. Each in turn merits attention, a multi-vocal sequence.

The Chaucer of the General Prologue bows in as though the group pilgrimage were coincidence of time and place:

> Bifel that in that seson on a day . . .
> as I lay
> Redy to wenden on my pilgrymage . . .
> At nyght was come into that hostelrye
> Wel nyne and twenty in a compaignye . . .
> and pilgrimes were they alle . . .

Fortuitously, as would appear, Chaucer is so summoned to become literary gallery-maker and 'in accordaunt to resoun' summoned 'To telle yow al the condicioun/ Of ech of hem, so as it seemed to me'. The latter phrase aptly underscores the imaginative tactics in play. This will be Chaucer 'reasonably' summoned to inscribe journey and journeyers (himself included) and impelled to do so on best affecting terms. Ovid, Petrarch or Boccaccio he can acknowledge as high literary reference, but his tales draw upon 'sondry' English kind and in duly modern format.

The luminaries, spanning the admired 'parfit gentil knight' to the egregious and effeminate 'gentil pardoner', he artfully insists be made subject to himself as chance recorder, mere onlooker. In effect his 'own' voice throughout the General Prologue is never less than textually discernible, archly reticent, full of apology for his ineptness of manner. The upshot is a Chaucer of one and several authorial inflections operating – can we again say modernly? – from within but from well beyond medieval auspices.

Duty done in the way of portrait ('Now have I toold you, shortly in a clause,/ Th'estaat, th'array, the nombre . . .'), there follows narrative

MODERNS – CHAUCER TO CONTEMPORARY FICTION

agenda. It comes accompanied by the plea, purportedly, to be further forgiven for deviation from the original stories and the usual idiom of their narration:

> But now is tyme to yow for to telle
> How that we baren us that ilke nyght,
> Whan we were in that hostelrye alyght;
> And after I wol I telle of our viage
> An al the remenaunt of oure pilgrimage.
> But first I pray yow, of youre courteisye,
> That ye n'arette it nat my vileynye,
> Thogh that I pleynely speke in this mateere,
> To telle yow hir woirdes and hir cheere,
> Ne thogh I speke hir wordes proprely.
> For this ye knowen al so wel as I,
> Whoso shal telle a tale after a man.
> He moot reherce as ny as evere he kan
> Everich a word, if it be in his charge,
> Al speke he never so rudeliche and large,
> Or ellis he moot telle his tale untrewe,
> Or feyne thyng, or fynde wordes newe.
> He may nat spare, althoug he were his brother;
> He moot as wel seye o word as another.

The passage points to the circumstantial Tabard 'hostelrye' as departure point for the pilgrim 'viage' ahead, and to the likely adjustments, even equivocations, of the storytelling involved. The excuse for any dips into vulgarity, on grounds that this is how the stories were first related ('n'arette it nat my vileynye'), has about it attractive disingenuity. Chaucer declares himself the good-faith amanuensis, if given to tales 'rudeliche and large' then only because the originals so mandate. 'Everich a word', accordingly, must be used to respect each tale's first telling. The risk, otherwise, is that of making it 'untrewe'. The show of resolve upon truth-to-source plays equivocation all ways, not least the author's clear self-awareness as to the un-fulfilability of 'gospel' re-telling of the stories offered by his cycle of pilgrim sub-authors.

'Wordes newe', or as the text says, 'o word as another' (one word as another), is precisely what Chaucer writes, less un-truth than truth made subject to his own re-ordering flights. These phrases reflect the prestidigitation of the *Tales*, the narrative riffs, stops and starts, asides, pilgrim spats, and never least, interruptions. Nonetheless Chaucer insists upon the pose of honest broker, faithful in his telling, no embroiderer. He will even invoke Christ and Plato as to the desiderata of fitting right word to truth, language the cousin to the deed, with a self-upbraid should he be thought to have given way to errors of decorum in introducing the pilgrims. His summary gives a highly dubious nod to his apparent expressive limitations:

My wit is short, ye may wel understonde. (27)

Who, in fact, speaks here? Chaucer himself, Chaucer in his persona of scribe, the Chaucer who will become the 'Chaucer' of the Host's demand for 'som deyntee thing' and to which his 'Sir Thopas' will be the response? Whichever it is, and whether the one or a ply of voices, the invitation to believe him short in 'wit' (knowledge, judgement, or above all, imagination) works persuasively to camouflage compositional finesse.[3]

Matters are not yet finished once past the Prologue. Chaucer, in due guise, weaves himself into the tales in a run of selective introductions and epilogues. These interventions not only assure impetus, conversational theatre, they augment his contribution as a kind of co-compère with the Host. They are first to be heard after the Knight's Tale when the Host, aided by the Monk and the Reeve, chastises the besotted Miller. The promise of a bawdy tale of cuckoldry, exposed rumps included, not only contrasts with the Knight's preceding courtly love-triangle story of Arcite, Palamon and Emily, it affords Chaucer a platform to re-enforce his posture of being obliged to transcribe in best suited idiom the scene as it has unfolded before him:

What sholde I moore seyn, but this Millere
He nolde his wordes for no man forbere,
But tolde his cherles tale in his manere.
M'athynketh that I shall reherce it heere.
And therfore every gentil wight I preye,
For Goddes love, demeth nat that I seye
Of yvel entente, but for I moot reherce
Hir tales alle, be they better or werse,
Or elles falsen some of my mateere.

> And thefore, whoso list it nat yheere,
> Turne over the leef and chese another tale . . .
> The Millere is a cherl, ye knowe wel this;
> So was the Reve, and othere manye mo,
> And harlotrie they tolden bothe two.
> Avyseth yow, and put me out of blame;
> And eek shal nat maken ernest of game.

The exculpatory ring once again flatters to deceive, the writer bound by fidelity to whatever vulgarities of circumstance or speech in the original; no fault his, it would appear. Miller and Reeve speak 'harlotrie' (here meaning ribaldry) as though operating beyond Chaucer's authorial control, the both of them churls, loose cannons. If they offend, runs the rubric, better to turn the page, choose another tale. These advertisements come hedged, knowing incitements to interest.

The author's rider of 'put me out of blame' speaks synoptically, Chaucer's staged haplessness in the face of having to respond to vernacular life lived and spoken. He even adds a writer-to-reader health warning not to be over-earnest in the matter of story as playfield ('and eek shall nat maken ernest of a game'). The manoeuvres all work to imaginative good purpose, Chaucer actively, and once again modernly, present in voice within the narrative grain of the text.

The self-participation in the *Tales* continues over into one other major interpolation, the 'Lenvoy de Chaucer' that follows the story of 'pacient Griselde' told by the Clerk of Oxenford. The account of the mean, capricious tests of loyalty put upon Griselde by her husband Walter, Marquis of Saluzzo, has its well-known source in Petrarch. As always Chaucer adapts his sources, as he does with the rest of the marriage group. Whether spoken *in propria persona* or in narrator voice, the Lenvoy gives a fiery smack at the misogyny and advocates fiercely for equal powers in human relationship ('Ne suffreth nat that men yow doon offense'). At the same time the Lenvoy acts quite in line with his other authorial markers, the writer as implicit co-player in his own text.

The rest of the marriage group gives confirmation. 'The Miller's Tale' circles narrative within narrative with its larky, mock-Flood sex-romp of Nicholas and Alison at the expense of the carpenter

Old John and the flouncing churchman Absolon. 'The Wife of Bath's Tale', hands-on fleshly repudiation of wifely submission, appropriates equal rights of telling as of female autonomy. 'The Merchant's Tale', with its January–May account, allows Chaucer to provide a bitter pointer to the teller of the tale's unharmonious late-in-life marriage. 'The Franklin's Tale', with its Brittany aristocratic story of Averagus, Dorigen and Aurelio as yet another love-triangle, turns queryingly on a test of women's fidelity in marriage. Chaucer ever gives notice of his presence.

The role of the Host throughout the Tales, beyond 'Sir Thopas', has connecting importance in how *The Canterbury Tales* pitches its 'modern' authoring. Brusque, hail-fellow, choirmaster and choir, in an evident sense he makes the perfect interlocutor. His role, however, extends into another *alter ego* voice. For in having the Host provide commentary, and orchestrate the running order, Chaucer cleverly again delegates his authorial standing. The Host, in other words, acts as surrogate, whether the 'semely man' of the General Prologue who proposes the pilgrim story-cycle, or the rapporteur and cajoler and then censor of the 'Chaucer' who offers 'the rym I lerned long agoon'.

In this latter instance, the 'murye' Host and the hangdog versifier who recites 'Sir Thopas' play each other's opposite and yet familiar. The Prologue's description of the Host as 'boold of his speche', 'wys' and 'wel ytaught', thereby, points well beyond incidental character detail. An altogether wider authorial reflection is indicated. That is, the Host not only solicits 'tales tweye' on the journey to and back from Canterbury, he equally shadows, and even appears to undermine, the true speaker-writer of the Tales.

In this role the Host assumes creative sway, at once acquisitions editor ('ech of yowe, to shorte with oure weye/ In this viage shal telle tales tweye') and authority ('oure governour'). He also will assume the role of the pilgrimage's literary critic-cum-historian, or as Chaucer designates him, 'of oure tales juge and reportour'. Once en route he reminds the company of the cost to querying his decisions ('Whoso be rebel to my juggement/ Shal paye for al that by the wey is spent'). His baton established, there remains only the narrative sequence of tales, the pilgrims to deliver on the sworn-to promise of a 'omposicioun' with the Host as redactor-general.

22 MODERNS – CHAUCER TO CONTEMPORARY FICTION

As the tales get told the Host, with a number of exceptions, audibly acts the enthusiast, disputant, cajoler, even revealer of secrets of his family life. He knows the social rules, first deference to the Knight ('my mayster and my lord,/ Now draweth cut, for that is myn accord') and courtesy to the religious ('Cometh neere . . . my lady Prioresse') or 'And ye, sire Clerk, lat be youre shamefacednesss,/ Ne studieth noght'). If Chaucer can play narrator at large, or in-house textual 'Chaucer', he at the same time accords the Host seeming responsibility for the entire *mise-en-scène*.

Subsequent exchanges confirm the Host continuing to act as though by authorial fiat. At the close of 'The Knight's Tale', which has won high approval, and with 'The Miller's Tale' still in prospect, it is the Host who contentedly summarises the state-of-play:

> This gooth aright; unbokeled is the male.
> Let se now who shal telle another tale;
> For trewely the game is wel bigonne.

If he thinks all is well, the storytelling 'unbuckled' from the 'male' (a bag), and his choice of the Monk as successor to the Knight, Chaucer knocks him off his editorial perch in the person of the Miller 'dronke of ale' and boozily contentious ('By armes, and by blood and bones,/ I kan a noble tale for the nones'). The Host is led into sparring with the Miller ('That I am dronke, I knowe it by my soun'). The Miller perfectly acknowledges that he might 'mysspeke' his carpenter story, or remonstrate with the Reeve as ex-carpenter. He readily throws in a few groundling bits of advice about not being too particular about God or wife. Chaucer, in another feint, even has to step in for the Host ('What sholde I seyn, but this Millere/ He nolde his wordes for no man forbere'). The voices nicely elide: the Host overmanned for once, Chaucer ('Chaucer') in customary apologetic mode for the sexual charade that is to follow:

> I moot reherce
> His tales alle, be they better or werse,
> Or elles falsen som of my mateere.

This makes for gamester art, Chaucer's modern parliament of contrary voice.

The Host's interventions continue. He reprimands the Reeve, Oswald, for his preacherly style as he seeks to get revenge on the

Miller in his counter-story of another miller, that of Symkyn, his wife and daughter, and the two Cambridge students. He mocks the Cook, Roger, for past culinary sharp practice, and is then himself mocked with the prospect of a story about a publican on the prospective return from Canterbury. In turning to the Man of Law he reminds him that it is his 'devoir' to offer a tale. The lawyer declares his storytelling limitations, however belied by the three-part story he tells of shipwreck, Christian conversion and kingship. In added commentary it is also the lawyer who offers pertinent observations on Chaucer's writing:

> I kan right now no thrifty tale seyn
> That Chaucer, though he kan but lewedly
> On metres and on rhyming craftily,
> Hath seyd them in swich Engliesh as he kan
> Of olde tyme, as knoweth many a man;
> And if he have noght seyd hem, leve brother,
> In o book, he hath seyd hem in another.

The storytelling wheel rebounds back upon itself – Chaucer to Host, Host to Lawyer, Lawyer to Chaucer (and he, subsequently to 'Chaucer'). The touch is adroit authorial roundabout, 'modern' in self-referring finesse.

In yet other interventions the Host keeps true to his shared speaker-writer role. Turning to the 'Parisshe Prest' he is countermanded by the Shipman, adamant that he wants no preachment. If 'The Tale of Thopas' sparks his wrath against 'Chaucer', the Host largely misunderstands 'The Tale of Melibee' as merely a piece of marriage-guidance applicable to his wife ('I hadde levere . . . that my wyf, hadede herd this tale!/ For she nys no thing of swych patience'). The Monk he seeks to cheer up ('be myrie of cheere'), advocating he take a wife and engage in procreation, then supports the Knight in cutting short his Tale's litany of the Great and Good. He celebrates 'The Nun's Priest's Tale' with its rooster Chanticleer, vents outrage at the corrupt and predatory judge-figure in 'The Physician's Tale', invites the Pardoner to tell his story of money as root of evil only to be exploitatively peddled a relic (and to find himself again infuriated and in need of being pacified by the Knight), and solicits from the Merchant yet another marriage tale. There remains for him to preside, briefly, over the Squire and Franklin for their tales.

In these different acts of co-authoring the Host gives continuum to the Tales, the necessary bridge narrator. He remains at all times Harry Bailey, taverner of Southwark, and at the same time acts true to his identity of Chaucer's emissary. The medieval modern of *The Canterbury Tales* in a prime orchestral sense relies upon him.

In none of this account should it be thought that Chaucer is to be de-historicised.[4] Demonstrably he draws from his time's milieu and language. His sources have been conscientiously excavated: Bible and Church literature, Hagiography, Latin and Greek classics, Boccaccio and contemporaries, Romance, European history (kingship to the crusades) and popular legend. At the same time he exhibits inerasable, one might say almost trans-historical, command. Self-circling, interjections, the willingness to interrogate one or another apparent authority of voice, all have their play.

For if 'the modern' is thought to reside in the grasp, and transformation, of the medieval world, that has much to do with Chaucer's varying range of voice. The 'Chaucer' of 'Sir Thopas' localises the achievement to perfection. The Prologue offers a model of authorial manoeuvre. The 'Lenvoy de Chaucer' has the author himself speak under the guise of homilist. The interventions of the Host monitor and extend the drama. The prefaces guide and on occasion tease the pilgrim stories to follow. Chaucer, in other words, displays bravura self-enrolment in the text. Therein, it would be fair to say he effects nothing other than the 'beste rym I kan' as his abiding 'modern' pathway.

Notes

1. *The Poetical Works of Chaucer*, ed. F. N. Robinson, Boston, MA: Houghton, Mifflin, 1933. Republished in The Cambridge Poets series, Oxford and New York: Oxford University Press, 1957. All references are to this latter edition. 'Heere taketh the makere of this booke his leve', 314.
2. The scholarship on 'The Tale of Sir Thopas' has been not inconsiderable. See, selectively, an early study like J. M. Manly, 'Sir Thopas, A Satire', which sees the story's main purpose to be the mockery of bourgeois Flemish pretension, *The Chaucer Review*, *Essays and Studies*, 13, 52–73, 1928; J. A. Burrow, 'Sir Thopas: An Agony in Three Fits', *Review of English Studies*, 22, 54–8, 1971; Ann S. Haskell, 'Sir Thopas: the Puppet's Puppet', *The Chaucer Review*, 9:3, 252–62,

CHAUCER AND 'SIR THOPAS'

1975; Glending Olson, 'Reading of the Thopas-Melibee Link', *The Chaucer Review*, 10, 147–53, 1975; David C. Benson, 'Their Telling Difference: Chaucer the Pilgrim and Two Canterbury Tales', *The Chaucer Review*, 18:1, 61–76, 1983; and Lee Patterson, '"What Man Artow?" Authorial Self-Definition in the *Tale of Sir Thopas* and *The Tale of Melibee*', *Studies in the Art of Chaucer*, 11, 117–75, 1989. See also Robert M. Correale and Mary Hamil (eds), *Sources and Analogues for The Canterbury Tales*, Cambridge: D. S. Brewer, Vol. 1, 2002; Vol. 2, 2005.

3. For an excellent analysis of Chaucer's tactics in *The Canterbury Tales*, see Gabriel Josipovici, 'Chaucer: The Teller and the Tale', 52–99, *The World and the Book*, London: Macmillan, 1971.

4. The classic study in this respect remains D. W. Robertson, *Preface to Chaucer: Studies in Medieval Perspectives*, Princeton, NJ: Princeton University Press, 1962. I also need to acknowledge the excellent reception study by Stephanie Trigg in *Congenial Souls: Reading Chaucer from Medieval to Postmodern*, Minneapolis: University of Minnesota Press, 2002.

CHAPTER 2

My Lady Mistress, Dame Philology: John Skelton

For Robert Graves in his *Oxford Addresses on Poetry* (1962), Skelton's 'Speke, Parrot' (1521) stands as 'the first modernist poem in English'.[1] It has not been a judgement that carries all before it. C. S. Lewis, in his role of ranking medievalist, ventured that Skelton was always of the lower tier, a first maybe but of 'the nonsense poets'.[2] Either way, would it not be anachronistic, wayward, to accord Skelton a modern silhouette given his rootedness in the fifteenth and sixteenth centuries as it steered from the late Middle Ages into the early Tudor Renaissance? Can this Skelton truly step forward from his time as courtier, priest, classicist and stickler for Catholic doctrine amid the rising energies of the Reformation? Whether salute or reservation, argument joins, the case for Skelton in whichever degree an early poet-practitioner of the modern.

To this end scrutiny has to go beyond Skelton's personal history or clerical politics to the poetics of his verse and most especially 'Speke, Parrot'. It also means re-visitation of poems like 'Phyllyp Sparow' (1508) with its implicit bordering of theology and erotica, flytings like 'The Bouge of Court' (1498), 'Why Come Ye Nat to Courte?' (1522–3) and 'Colyn Cloute' (1522), and the ceremonial 'The Garland of Laurel' (1523), which audaciously argues for Skelton's initiation into literature's hall of fame. In 'Speke, Parrot', however, the case for assigning Skelton place in a 'modern' roster remains at its most decisive.

Contempt for the arrogance of power personified in Cardinal Wolsey, and for the wider malfeasance of Tudor church and court, leaves no doubt of the targets. The critique Skelton offers, wholly trenchant although for tactical good reason guarded, also and equally wins effect in the manner of delivering his accusations. For the versification almost acrobatically gives performance to the

26

dissent, a calculated platform of voice. Nomination of Skelton as modern, or 'first modernist', resides here as much as elsewhere. Ian Alistair Gordon also sees in 'Speke, Parrot' anticipation of the polyphony of the modernist turn:

> The difficulty of *Speke Parrot* has obscured its amazing originality. Here in the first few years of the sixteenth-century is Skelton writing in an idiom of the twentieth ... his method of writing in *Speke Parrot* is disconcertingly close to that of T.S. Eliot and Ezra Pound, and emphasizes the allusive bias of mind of Skelton.[3]

The observation turns on how Skelton's indictment of Wolsey and the politics in his name draws force exactly from the poem's compositional means. For it points to the Skelton beyond tutorship of the prince who will become Henry VIII, or his tenure of laureateships from both Oxford and Cambridge, or his besiegement in Westminster Abbey, or his legendary garrulousness as Vicar of Diss, or even his repute as the scourge of Wolsey. Opinion rightly has settled on the poem as Skelton's best configuration and trope. The invocation in 'Speke, Parrot' of 'Dame Philology' and her 'gifté ... to learn all language' gives the pointer. However historically situated, or even sealed, 'Speke, Parrot' in its wide allusive reference along with associated riddles, matches disdain for the bad faith of his era's governance with the strength – and modernity – of his poetics.

Any proposal of Skelton as modern has to deal with the eclecticism of his learning, Latin or Greek, biblical or secular. That might be challenge enough. But despite C. S. Lewis's unfavouring estimate, Skelton invites acknowledgement for his formidable literary-linguistic creativity. Old English alliteration, kennings, his versatility with the skeltonic as it has come to be known, play their part, albeit servants not masters. 'Nonsense poet' does not really come close to fitting the bill. Skelton goes well beyond mere acoustics, antic wordplay.

'Colyn Clout', as a first instance, works not just to attack the episcopacy of Wolsey and clerical fault lines in general. It does so as if to throw Skelton's very poetics in the reader's face. Clout's

28 MODERNS – CHAUCER TO CONTEMPORARY FICTION

stroppy insistence on his identity, and his combative rhyme, has about it a near-physical quality:

> And if ye stand in doubt
> Who brought this rhyme about,
> My name is Colin Clout.

The poem displays self-referencing at the outset:

> What can it avail . . .
> To rhyme or to rail,
> To write or to indict,
> Either for delight
> Or else for despite?
> Or bookes to compile
> Of divers manner style,
> Vice to revile
> And sin to exile?

Skelton clearly knows 'what it can avail' to confront the church's venality. More still he knows how to deploy authoring to meet the task. With Thomas à Becket named for moral fulcrum, the poem lists instances of errant behaviour to include 'Prelacy bought and sold', cash-on-demand 'dispensations', and 'schismatics' of the kind associated in his own time with Wycliffe, Tyndale and Luther. The accusation also points up 'polluted' language, Christianity's true doctrine of 'the word' traduced whether from pulpit or in general clerical practice. This, as the poem goes on to insist, is to contrast the acquisitive present with the godly eternal dimension or in the church's Latin *in secular seculorum*.

It is against these betrayals that Clout, and Skelton behind him, posits his poetics when he says 'Make ye no murmuration,/ Though I write after this fashion'. Churchly falling-away conjoins with dissident literary satire:

> I purpose to shake out
> All my conning bag
> Like a clerkly hag.
> For though my rhyme be ragged,
> Tattered and jagged,

Rudely rain-beaten,
Rusty and moth-eaten,
If ye take well therewith,
It hath in it some pith.

Thrust and repetition become the poem's very measure ('Say this, and say that'). Beat of rain, rust, even the gnaw of moths and bad weather supply winning metaphors.

Further irony suffuses the wry closing regret that the 'book' in likelihood is destined not 'printed for to be' on grounds of dissidence, refusal to acquiesce. The decision likely involves a hedge against persecution by the Wolsey entourage. All that remains is 'Now to withdraw my pen'. The paradox of Skelton's volubility being put under restraint, self-denying ordinance, foreshadows one other aspect of the modern, namely the author as adept in James Joyce's 'silence, exile, and cunning'.[4] The charge, sometimes, has gone up of doggerel, jingle over sense. That does injustice. Skelton's poetics deserve better, assuredly not those of Gerard Manley Hopkins with whom he shares a style of accentual pattern, nonetheless perfectly striking.

'Speke, Parrot' signifies Skelton's largest exercise of imagination but his yet other better-known verse help place the poem. Feints and counter-feints point the way. Sonic language-play contributes. In these respects 'The Bouge of Court', his arraignment of the buying and selling of influence in court and country, comes early into play. 'I call to mind the great authority/ Of poets old' runs the poem at the outset, aligning the speaker's work with the practice of earlier satirists who have used 'covert terms' and cloaked truth 'subtilly'.

The ensuing stanzas almost revel in ironic faux-modesty, the speaker rounding on himself for lack of qualification on account of his 'to-dull' ability and being subject to 'Ignorance . . . advising me my pen away to pull,/ And not to write'. Fortunately, or so it is alleged, dream comes to the rescue, the vision of a ship bearing goods that will curry favour with the royal court. This opening marks authorship fully willing to acknowledge its reflexive wrap: the hapless versifier compelled to utterance by the random sighting of a ship seen 'at Harwich port', satirist and his satire animated by

30   MODERNS – CHAUCER TO CONTEMPORARY FICTION

mere freak of occasion. Skelton allows his mask, his late medieval modern, just to slip sufficiently.

'Why Come Ye Not to Court?' again engages in shrewd poetics, the speaker-persona, the line of interrogation. The answer to the mock ingenuous question of the title involves shies at both corrupt prelacy, with Wolsey as always the chief offender, and at the consenting and abetting landed gentry. Has not the one-eyed Cardinal ('The Devil's Vicar General') usurped royal powers, taken hold of the kingdom by stealth? The satire is learned, scriptural and historic, and abrim in classical citation from Juvenal to Petrarch. The poem is also fully aware of, and shrewdly willing to signal, its own imaginative devising.

The opening lines, beginning in the imperative, dare the reader to avoid paying attention:

> Mark well this conclusion . . .
> A nobleman may fall,
> And his honour appal;
> And if you think this shall
> Not rub you on the fall
> Then the devil take all!

Expansively the poet seeks to make sure the reader-at-large is on notice to give full attentive ear to the arising serial of questions in the form of *What newes, what newes?* and *What hear ye of . . .?* The issues range through derelictions to do with a local bawdy house as symptom of things bought and sold, aristocratic miscreancy in Lancashire, Cheshire and Scotland, political villainy by Lord Dacres, Lord Rose and the King of Scotland, apprehension about the intention of Burgundians and the French fleet, and sight of the Red Hat of Wolsey as symbol of power and its abuse.

Other indictments follow, all we are enjoined to believe, in need of wider hearing:

> Hereafter perchance I shall
> Make a larger memorial
> And a further rehearsal,
> And more paper I think to blot,
> To the court why I come not;
> Desiring you above all thing
> To keep you from laughing

> When you fall to reading
> Of this wanton scroll . . .

At every turn the text patrols itself. 'Further rehearsal', blotted paper, and eye-catchingly, 'this wanton scroll', bespeak the very implements of authoriality, the writer at his cyphering workbench. The prospective 'larger memorial' implies composition still to be folded into those already written, meta-inscription wholly familiar in kind to readers of the modern.

'The Garland of Laurel' draws many of these features into another single and considerably extensive thread. In having Yorkshire's Sheriff Hutton Castle and the Forest of Galtres transpose into a Palace of Art presided over by the Countess of Surrey and her daughters, Skelton creates the perfect fabular scene for his own would-be literary laurels. The garland of embroidered silk, and gold and pearls, leads into literary-genealogical affiliation, among others, with Ovid, Juvenal, Aristotle, Diogenes, Cicero, Plutarch and Petrarch. The Gods themselves are to be heard debating Skelton's own merit. The earthly honour roll, duly embellished in deific and heraldic allusion, moves onwards to the figure of SKELTON POETA. Most of all he is to be affiliated with his English compeers:

> I saw Gower, that first garnished our English rude,
> And Master Chaucer, that nobly enterprised
> How that our English might freshely be enewed;
> The monk of Bury then after them ensued,
> Dan John Lydgate: these English poetes three,
> As I imagined, repaired after me . . .

Fellow 'English poetes three' and others speak to him directly, Skelton's fond sharers of the laurel. He gives tactful dedications to the leading ladies of his time, recapitulates his own work, and offers an Envoy as to how his life, not to say reputation, hovers in the balance given Wolseyite threat ('Take no depair/ Though I you wrate' and 'I drede ye shall have need . . . to speed . . . against envy and obloquy'). Above all, this is Skelton writing, or more precisely writing himself in, as self-figuring reflection, pitched to see himself at the helm of literary-creative fellowship.

32   MODERNS – CHAUCER TO CONTEMPORARY FICTION

Scholarship has given a fair amount of attention to 'Speke, Parrot'. It has featured as 'self-consuming artefact' (Stanley Fish), been seen for its part in the early Renaissance wars of Latin as against Greek (A. R. Heiserman), and been annotated in relation to Christian theology (Arthur F. Kinney) and Tudor politics (Greg Walker).[5] These have their admirable synopsis in Jane Griffiths's *John Skelton and Poetic Authority: Defining the Liberty to Speak* (2006), with its exploration of how Skelton seeks his 'authorization' as poet.[6] The account establishes a Skelton far more in the round, be it time-and-place court politics or the evolving nuances of his Christianity. 'Speke, Parrot', despite being Skelton's generally agreed centrepiece, has not resisted cavils. He is said to risk obfuscation, too elusive an overall knot. The fuller implications of granting it modern/modernist status, even so, remain.

At the outset, and mindful that the title is in fact an imperative, how not to relish the trope of the poet as parrot given new flair, even exoticism?

> My name is Parrot, a bird of Paradise,
> By nature devised of a wonderous kind,
> Daintily dieted with divers delicate spice
> Till Euphrates, that flood, driveth me into Ind;
> Where men in that country by fortune me find
> And send me to greate ladyes of estate:
> Then Parrot must have an almond or a date.

'Wonderous' could not better suit. Paradisal, spice-fed, Mesopotamian, river-brought to India and thence to the west as trophy, the bird's itinerary is as full-blown imaginary as literally geographic. That Parrot requires the care of ladyship and to be fed the delicacy of almond or date adds credential to its individual deserving. Detail accumulates of its 'curiously carven' cage, 'silver pin', 'couveryure', and the attentive cooing it stirs. Appearance carries stature, whether curved beak, 'wanton' eye, emerald green feathering, or ruby proportioned neck. The sum, mock-modest as it were, leads into the vaunt 'I am a minion to wait upon a queen'. More to the point, schooled alongside the well-bred ladies who give him coddling, Parrot has become the doyen of multiple languages.

This transition to the bird's vocal stamp is crucial, 'parroting' as the poet's throat for speaking out in the world despite stricture or even outright censorship, and given to doing so under seeming ostentatious

JOHN SKELTON   33

but actually hidden authorial cover. In no time the poly-lingualism embraces Latin, Hebrew, Arabic, Chaldean, Greek. The 'modern' languages follow, whether French with its demand for correctness ('*Parlez bien*, Parrot, *ou parlez rien!*'), Spanish with its gesture to Katherine of Aragon ('*sabe hablar Castiliano*'), or the German revealed in a subsequent stanza with its allusions to *lieber Got von Himmelsreich*. The semi-cascade, along with the reported blessings of Henry VIII, the attribution of the parrot's language gifts to 'Dame Philology', and aphorisms in Latin like '*Moderata juvant*' ('Moderation delights'), spurs Parrot's further ironic self-reprobation. 'Parrot, *par ma foi:/ Taisez-vous . . . tenez vous coy*' rounds the upbraid, the seeming prattler telling itself to quieten the volume.

Throughout there can be no mistaking the parrot's having been summoned to disempower Wolsey's grip over Henry's kingdom. *Ich dien*, the heraldic German 'I serve' of Henry VIII when still Prince of Wales, fuses into that of the bird. Recondite as may now be the allusions, whether biblical or folk-popular, the aim stays fixed on Wolsey as Judas Iscariot. Skelton can use the ostensible gush of the bird's 'parroting', that of seeming popinjay, the mere court toy, as his surrogate, but it is an impersonation that has the dividend of genuine inventiveness. For he maintains his parrot-speech with fine touch, that of his own kind of modern.

He has the bird first launch into self-colloquy, speaker and spoken to ('*Que pensez-vous, Parrot?* what meaneth this business?'). Invoking Old Testament prophets, Aaron and Job, the parrot contrasts as it were its own inebriated folderol with these biblical worthies ('Peace, Parrot, ye prate as ye were *ebrius*'). Additional comment is drawn from Scots and Welsh vernacular, the parrot speaking at one and the same time as at-risk orator ('ware the false cat') in the London ('Esebon') controlled by Wolsey ('Og'). Invoking an anthology like Albertus's *Margarita Poetica* (1472), with its rhetorical protocols, Skelton takes a further pivot and plays the loquacity of the parrot against its author's politically suppressed tongue in the lines 'I pray you, let Parrot have liberty to speak!' and 'Let Parrot, I pray you, have liberty to prate'. These contrasts and overlaps continue in kind.

On the one hand there is the parrot as popinjay, the fluttery show-off:

'Parrot, Parrot, Parrot, pretty popinjay!'
       With my beak I can pick my little pretty toe:

34   MODERNS – CHAUCER TO CONTEMPORARY FICTION

My delight is solace, pleasure, disport, and play.
    Like a wanton, when I will, I reel to and fro.
Parrot can say *Caesar, ave*! also.
But Parrot hath no favour to Esebon.
Above all other birdes, set Parrot alone.

On the other hand the parrot positions itself with other would-be truthsayers against political bad faith (Wolsey again), fake science ('chiromancy'), the abandonment of Greek for Latin ('*aurea lingua Graeca* ought to be magnified'), and the reduction of scholarship ('Parrot the popinjay hath pity to behold/ How the rest of good learning is roufled up and trold'). The balance is purposely struck, plaything and seer.

Skelton has the Parrot insist on itself as no mere 'woodcock' or 'starling' but 'popinjay royall'. It can look to immortality ('When Parrot is dead she does not putrify'). The bird so stands within and outside itself, the abiding and 'peerless' witness to the eventual 'dust' of things ('Pomp, pride, honours, riches'). The final appeal gives both writer and reader equal participant rights of witness:

Thus Parrot doth pray you,
With heart most tender,
To reckon with this recueil now,
And it to remember.

Skelton and parrot, author and persona, with the reader expressly invited into the liaison, locates the poem's overall strategy. The sum carries its flair severally: satire, mask, subversion, sound, and for sure, intimations of the modern.

In the sequences that round out the poem the parrot becomes an almost free-floating spirit, polyglot lyricist to the Ovidian sea-nymph Galathea, speaker of a half-dozen 'envois', and finally, ruminative soliloquist. The recapitulation that is offered does typical duty, retrospect and challenge:

Thus much Parrot hath openly expressed.
Let see who dare make up the rest.

Aim is so taken at 'one and other at me that have disdain' and those who 'say, I rail at riot reckless'. A skeltonic barrage ensues indicting 'causeless cowards', 'manless manhood', 'conning clergy'. Skelton's modern-sounding cascade un-abates.

On being offered 'a date' by Galathea to 'speak', the parrot fires more cannonade against the 'franticness' of Wolsey's regime of 'jumble', 'stumble', 'tumble'. Galathea is to be imagined asking for 'true and plain' speech, an invitation the parrot could not more welcome in its lamentation at an age deemed 'hardy dardy', 'prodigal', given over to 'gee-gaw' and 'so little perfite truth'. The aristocracy has become 'dull', the church 'shameful' display and corruption. Wolsey's seizure of undue power, that of the reputed son of a butcher, elicits memorable contempt ('So fat a maggot, bred of fleshés-fly').

In all, runs the parrot's summary, 'Since Deucalion's flood the world was never so ill'. The flyting ends in a literally paired signing-off – '*Dixit*, quod Parrot' and 'Quod Skelton, Laureat, *Orator Regius*'. The elision of the two makes for perfect leave-taking, the one register folded into the other. It marks nothing other than Skelton's double-tongued 'modern' hail and farewell to 'Speke, Parrot'.

Avian tropes mount to a considerable genealogy in English-language verse. Chaucer's bird-gathering dream poem *Parlement of Foules* contributes an early marker. The English Romantics yield Keats's nightingale and its music, Shelley's skylark and its blithe spirit, and Coleridge's albatross slain and hung about the neck of the mariner-penitent. In America Poe imagines his death-raven, Wallace Stevens his conjugation of thirteen blackbirds. Among kindred compositions Thomas Hardy's darkling thrush serves as emblem of old and incoming century, Yeats's fifty-nine wild swans at Coole of love's remembrance, and Ted Hughes's hawk in the rain of the primal equation of raptor and hunted. It may be contentious though no disservice to associate Skelton's parrot with the lineage. E. M. Forster certainly thought to put him there:

> Speke Parrot – yet another bird: had Skelton a bird complex? Ornithologists must decide – Speke Parrot is one of those convenient devices where Polly is made to say what Polly's master hesitates to say openly.[7]

36 MODERNS – CHAUCER TO CONTEMPORARY FICTION

Without suggesting that there has been conscious borrowing, other footfalls of 'Speke, Parrot' bear the echo. One can cite Sidney Keyes, Robert Graves's fellow war poet albeit of World War II, in 'The Parrot':

> The bird speaks right tonight: my talking bird
> Of blood attacks his cage, shouting our secrets.
> His wisdom slapdash, he announces
> Interpretation crooked – . . .
> Speak bird. Speak parrot. Speak, then,
> Heart in the night from your elaborate
> Cage of white ribs: cry and defy decorum.[8]

The Welsh poet Dannie Abse in 'Talking to Myself' also emulates Skelton, the parrot trope again as human loquacity:

> Quick quick
> speak, old parrot,
> do I not feed you with my life?[9]

The wider inclusion, with the parrot as centrepiece, embraces Flaubert's 'Un Coeur Simple' and its dazzling follow-through in Julian Barnes's novel of truth and mirror in *Flaubert's Parrot* (1984). Pertinently Joseph Conrad can be summoned from *Under Western Eyes* (1911) in the observation, 'To a teacher of languages there comes a time when the world is but a place of many words and man appears a mere talking animal not much more wonderful than a parrot.'[10] As far away as Japan, Kazuko Shiraishi in the poem 'Parrot' avails herself of a share in the trope:

> I said 'I love you.'
> You answered, 'I love you.'
> I said 'I hate you.'
> You answered, 'I hate you.'
> I said, 'Shall we separate now?'
> You answered, 'Shall we separate now?'
> Always, always.
> You were a parrot.
> It was because you repeated my words exactly
> That we came to separate.[11]

JOHN SKELTON   37

Tudor John Skelton to present-century Julian Barnes, England's Skelton to Japan's Shiraishi? The notion attracts even as it teases, a conjoined 'modern' line of descent. For 'Speke, Parrot', from its distance in the literary timeline and amid its hugely allusive and even arcane skeins of learning, delivers also the speech of nearness. The poem steers beyond the classical allusion, the colloquial argot, the skeltonic, into performance for more than any one season. Satire it may be but the label goes only a certain distance. Skelton, rather, writes a poem whose lien on the modern 'speaks' well, and memorably, in anticipation of that of later ages.

Notes

1. Robert Graves, *Oxford Addresses on Poetry*, New York: Doubleday, 1962, 31. Graves's well-known fondness is equally to be found in his poem 'John Skelton', *Poems 1914–26*, London: William Heinemann, 1927. The relevant lines read:

   Tenderly, prettily,
   Laughingly, learnedly,
   Sadly, madly,
   Helter-skelter John
   Rhymes serenely on,
   As English poets should.
   Old John, you do me good!

2. For the fuller account, see C. S. Lewis, *English Literature in the Sixteenth Century*, Oxford: The Clarendon Press, 1944. 'This raises in some minds', he observes, 'the question of whether we are reading the first of the nonsense poets, or whether Skelton is anticipating the moderns and deliberately launching poetry on the "stream of consciousness". I believe not . . . Our pleasure in it may be almost wholly foreign to Skelton's purpose . . . The things that Mr Graves got out of Skelton's work are much better than anything Skelton put in.' 141–3.

3. Ian Alistair Gordon, *John Skelton: Poet Laureate*, Melbourne: Melbourne University Press, 1943, 161.

4. James Joyce, *A Portrait of the Artist as a Young Man*, 1916. Reprinted New York: The Viking Press, 1956, 247. The words, to be sure, are spoken not in Joyce's first person but by Stephen Daedalus.

5. These, respectively, are as follows: Stanley Fish, *John Skelton's Poetry*, New Haven, CT: Yale University Press, 1965, *Self-Consuming Artefacts: The Experience of Seventeenth Century Literature*, Berkeley:

38   MODERNS – CHAUCER TO CONTEMPORARY FICTION

The University of California Press, 1972; A. R. Heiserman, *Skelton and Satire*, Chicago: University of Chicago Press, 1961; Arthur F. Kinney, *Humanist Poetics: Thought, Poetics, Rhetoric, and Fiction in 16th Century England*, Amherst: University of Massachusetts Press, 1986; and Greg Walker, *John Skelton and the Politics of the 1520s*, New York: Cambridge University Press, 2002.

6. Jane Griffiths, *John Skelton and Poetic Authority: Defining the Liberty to Speak*, New York: Oxford University Press, 2006.

7. E. M. Forster, 'John Skelton', *Two Cheers for Democracy*, London: Edward Arnold, 1951. Republished London: Penguin Books, 1965, 151.

8. Sidney Keyes, 'The Parrot', *The Collected Poems of Sidney Keyes*, London and New York: Routledge, 1988.

9. Dannie Abse, 'Talking to Myself', *Speak Old Parrot*, London: Hutchinson, 2013, 2.

10. Joseph Conrad, *Under Western Eyes*, reprinted London and New York: Penguin Books, 1979, 55.

11. Kazuko Shiraishi, 'Parrot', *Seasons of Sacred Lust*, New York: New Directions, 1978, 34.

CHAPTER 3

Mind's Eye: *Hamlet* and Modernity

To be or not to be. Few locutions more reverberate down the corridors of English literature. Is not this Hamlet's summary call to consciousness of life's alpha and omega? What are the operative terms of being and non-being? Who am I? To say these interrogations lie stunningly embedded in the soliloquy's opening syllables is also to give points of compass for how *Hamlet* holds ground as one of the great literary benchmarks in the formulation of the modern.[1]

That is the question. The remaining half-line, as indeed the rest of the soliloquy in the interlinking sequence of 'sleep', 'dream', 'resolution' and 'thought', carries nothing if not our modern/ modernist sense of the self's interiority, its existential gyre. That Shakespeare finds wording so exactly abbreviated, and in speech rhythm to match, gives the line added and inerasable memorability. For the legacy of *To be or not to be* is incontestably immense, long having become *une expression fixe* in English usage and as frequent as any in its repetition.

Commentary, frequent to a fault, has come from sometimes unlikely sources. Jack Kerouac in *Desolation Angels* (1965) gives a Zen substratum to Shakespeare's line with 'To be *and* not to be, that's what we are'.[2] The narrator in Ian McEwan's novel *Saturday* (2005), speaking of the surgeon protagonist as 'waiting to see what he will do next', bears pertinently upon Hamlet's self-queries as to what he is, or might be, or can be, should he take on the injunction called for by his father's ghost.[3] Richard Berengarten, poet, in *A Portrait in Interviews* (2017) astutely underlines how *Hamlet* writes 'consciousness' into the Renaissance 'space' of inner selfhood and its turnings:

> Imagine a time before *Hamlet* was written. It's almost as though once it was written it enters into some kind of space that is, as it were, elemental, fundamental, as far as consciousness is concerned.[4]

39

40 MODERNS – CHAUCER TO CONTEMPORARY FICTION

These each in their different manner offer enlightening coordinates. Of Shakespeare's contemporaries, Montaigne in 'Que sais-je?'perhaps best contributes to how this modernity of self is to be understood. Of the more than a hundred *essaies*, begun in 1571 and selectively first published in 1580, few do keener service than 'Que sais-je?', which first appears in 'Apologie de Raymond Sebond'. His bid to get at the particularity of human experience rebuts any prompt to facile summary or categorisation. Admirers of Montaigne from Bacon to Hazlitt, Sainte-Beuve to Nietzsche, understandably were drawn to his acuity in this respect. How to address the world without reduction and how to address the self in the world? Byron adds his name to the questioners in *Don Juan* (1819–24) when he has his narrator observe '"To be or not to be?" – Ere I decide,/ I should be glad to know that which *is being*'.[5]

Later readers of Montaigne give confirmation. Erich Auerbach in *Mimesis: The Representation of Reality in Western Literature* (1946) sees in Montaigne the exploration of 'making oneself at home in existence without fixed points of support' and lauds the fact that 'for the first time, man's life – the random personal life as a whole – becomes problematic in the modern sense'.[6] Eric Hoffer, America's longshoreman philosopher, offers as witness to Montaigne in *Truth Imagined* (1983) the succinct 'He knew my innermost thoughts'.[7] The linkage of 'Que sais-je?' to 'To be or not to be', and of Auerbach and Hoffer back to Montaigne as Shakespeare's contemporary inquiring spirit, gives symptomatic albeit still selective genealogy to understanding the 'modern' condition.

This notion of the self of emergent modernity in *Hamlet* is hardly fortuitous given the European Renaissance and its bold illuminations of self in the world. Whether the *Hamlet* of the First Quarto (1603), then of the Second Quarto (1604–5) and the First Folio (1623), both the character and the play in which he is lodged could not more summon attention. For at almost every turn, and rarely more so than in the soliloquies, Hamlet like the speaker in Montaigne's essays recognises the theatre of himself, the conscious actor-*auteur* of self.[8]

As for the first time in English literature a work of imagination embodies in its principal figure the human mind, the human consciousness, appetitive (and not to say in Hamlet's case accusatory) in its own contemplation. 'An Outsider in his Own Life' serves as Morris Dickstein's title for a review of *Samuel Beckett: The Last*

Modernist (1997) by Anthony Cronin in the *New York Times*. The phrasing offers another bearing upon Hamlet as auto-chorus as he negotiates the call-to-action ghosted to him by his murdered father.[9]

That the amount of interpretation stirred by *Hamlet* exceeds that of any other Shakespeare play does not surprise. The cause goes infinitely beyond excavation of sources like the Amleth of *Historia Danica* by the medieval chronicler Saxo Grammaticus or the revenge-figure in one of the component stories of *Histoires Tragiques* by François de Belleforest. Equally it recognises that the play considerably exceeds analogies in Thomas Kyd's *The Spanish Tragedy* and the Middleton-Tourneur collaborative writing of *The Revenger's Tragedy*. *Hamlet* catches at the very axis of the self in examination of its own defining qualities, the synaptic processes of individual mind as it finds itself endeavouring to decipher reality.

Who, too, would not readily acknowledge the interpretative lineage of play and prince in English and American criticism? Dr Johnson avers that 'we must allow to the tragedy of *Hamlet* the praise of variety'. Coleridge is drawn to Hamlet's mind ('we see a great, an almost enormous intellectual activity'). T. S. Eliot, famously invoking the lack of 'objective correlative', insists that 'Hamlet the man is dominated by an emotion . . . in *excess* of the facts as they appear'. Harold Bloom, with typical brio, alleges that 'The play's subject is neither mourning for the dead nor revenge on the living . . . All that matters is Hamlet's consciousness of his own consciousness, infinite, unlimited, and at war with itself.' This latter interpretation almost but not quite coincides with the emphasis in the present account on the ways *Hamlet* gives meaning to 'the modern'.[10]

Actor-incarnations of the prince down history, Richard Burbage or David Garrick, Laurence Olivier or Kenneth Branagh, likewise have sought to bring understanding of the Hamlet who at quite the same time always also 'plays' himself. In this the relevance of how *Hamlet* as a work of theatre mirrors itself in Hamlet's instructions to the players of the Gonzago-Baptista story is not to be missed. The dumb-show wordlessly speaks its accusation as prologue to spoken enactment with the prince as participant scriptwriter, voice-coach and stage director.

Be it close reading of the page or stage performance, and beyond the plot line of usurpation and would-be revenge, the play persists through generation for generation in establishing grounds for its modernity.[11] That has held from the Romantic-age profile of Hamlet as tragically besieged 'character' through, latterly, to both Freudianism's son spooked by mother-love and New Historicism's 'political' prince situated inside the power play of a Scandinavian court which, however distantly, refracts England's transition from Tudor to Jacobean monarchy. Hamlet in fact can be seen to have given rise to a condition – Hamletism, debilitating self-awareness, the inability to transpose thought into action.[12] We can even resort for a gloss to so stupendously malign a spirit as Joseph Goebbels who designated Shakespeare, and quite especially *Hamlet*, 'more modern than the moderns'.[13]

'Let us impart what we have seen tonight/ unto young Hamlet' (I. i). Horatio so acts to further launch action that will border on parodying itself, namely Hamlet's sustained inaction. The opening points of departure give due premonition: midnight bell, winter chill, Bernardo, Francisco and Marcellus as change of watch, King Hamlet as armour-clad ghost, Horatio as at first sceptical witness, dawn's cock-crow, and the murdered king's command to revenge by the son to whom he bequeaths his name. The terms could not be more emphatic. Hamlet is to redress the assassination of his father and the incest he attributes to his mother, not to mention his disinheritance from the crown. Yet as much as Hamlet finds himself mandated to counter Claudius, be it by immediacy of rapier or possibly his own use of ear poison, the action will perversely become serial delay, the de-acceleration that comes from the overwhelming press of mind.

For whether in quietude or excitation Hamlet moves inward, into soliloquy, the mental arsenal from which he delivers each appraisal of his own indecision. Inherent, too, are his flurries of marauding wit, the sense of keeping at bay that 'Denmark's a prison' (II.i) and not just as locale but as language corridor of mendacity and false-dealing. Claudius or Gertrude, Polonius or Ophelia, Rosencrantz or Guildenstern, he addresses each as though speaking not just to or of them but in sardonic observance of the gap between things said and things meant. His own language adopts a passive-aggressive fount of ambiguity, euphemism, the one meaning tactically embedded inside the other. Only Horatio, astute confidant, manages best access to

Hamlet's visionary wordplay: 'He waxes desperate with imagination' (I.iv) gives the pointer.

The foundations for this self-monitoring play of language enter early. Faced with reprimand from his mother that 'all lives must die' and her disingenuous question 'Why seems it so particular with thee?' Hamlet rounds on her with symptomatic sleight of word. In scorn he plays bitterly on seem and be, from 'I know not "seems"' to 'I have that within which passes show' (I.ii). The speaking equivocates brilliantly, whether the actuality or metaphor of mourning clothes ('the trappings and the suits of woe') or the double-skein of his indictment of Claudius and Gertrude ('a little more than kin, and less than kind'). The supreme non-taker of action, he sees himself roiled in disturbed awareness of 'the actions that a man might play' (I.ii). Among them is his cruelty to Ophelia.

A keystone in his manner of circling back into the processes of his own mind arises in 'O, that this too too sullied flesh would melt' (I.ii), the first of the soliloquies. Here, and throughout its acclaimed tropes, Hamlet is to be met in passionate self-interrogation. Belief prohibits suicide. The world can be likened to a reverse Eden, an 'unweeded garden'. Womanhood, in the person of his mother, has become sexual 'frailty'. 'Incestuous sheets' succeed right parentage. Reason has fractured. Yet he, most articulate of men, for the moment and in the circumstances about him, 'must hold my tongue' (I.ii). As speaker Hamlet could not be more caught up in the materiality of word over action, modernly self-aware and indeed conscious of consciousness itself.

This pattern folds into Hamlet's almost every act of speech, those explicitly given to self-inquiry or in verbal exchanges with others. So energetic a language within language, articulacy that mirrors itself, however, has the effect of disruptive flux. It monitors itself to the point where it undermines any likelihood of intended revenge. In a perverse reversal of category, *Hamlet* could easily be thought the apogee of non-revenge tragedy whatever the final demise of Claudius among the play's final aggregation of the Danish court's dead.[14]

The play, or Hamlet's role within it, in a wholly primary way becomes the performance of what it is to have the mind recognise its own contrariety. That is not to suggest the eclipse of each other

44 MODERNS — CHAUCER TO CONTEMPORARY FICTION

interwoven theme. Quite the contrary. Love, the most powerful of human emotions, becomes its own fault line. Passion turns into riddle, whether Hamlet for his mother (and even his father) or Gertrude for her two husbands. Love of Ophelia segues into embitterment and his command to her to step from court to 'nunnery' if she is to escape the world's taint or even join it if we are to take nunnery to mean brothel. Death likewise overlaps throughout, King Hamlet's killing, Polonius's arras stabbing, Ophelia's drowning, the graveyard musings over Yorick's skull, the final catastrophe of rapier and duel. Power politics give another linkage as manifested in the Denmark and even Norway regimes. The terms are wholly appropriate and insistent: conspiracy, murder, usurpation, ceremony, the succession to the throne of Fortinbras, all played through and against Hamlet's observer-participant filter.

Family also threads necessarily into this *mise-en-scène*, be it fratricide ('by a brother's hand, of life, of crown, of queen at once dispatched' I.v), Gertrude's haste to re-marriage ('Hamlet, thou hast thy father much offended'./ 'Mother you have my father much offended' III.iv), or the faux respect of Claudius ('''Tis sweet and commendable in your nature, Hamlet, to give these mourning duties to your father' I.ii). Polonius can give plausible counsel both to Laertes ('above all, to thine own self be true', I.iii) and Ophelia ('Be somewhat scanter of your maiden presence' I.ii), yet show himself wholly self-availing in the espionage which leads to his death (Hamlet's 'fishmonger', II.ii, and 'rat', III.iv). The play incorporates these latitudes with a full hand.

Throughout, however, it is Hamlet's taking cognisance of his own thought, his intellection, that insistently gives centre to the play. Consciousness encloses and stalks. Unable to enact revenge, Hamlet gives way to the substitute circlings of thought, at one moment voluble, even manic, at another oddly becalmed. The ghost itself, although first sighted by the soldiery of the watch and by Horatio, Hamlet asserts to have had its prior existence 'in my mind's eye' (I.ii). His father is thus for him chimera but imagined for wholly real. Words, as he deploys them, increasingly spin and run in his attempt to control the unravelling world about him.

When, for instance, Laertes advises Ophelia that Hamlet's will 'is not his own' he ostensibly is referring to 'royal birth' and the high duties the prince will be required to perform which could put him out of her reach (I.iii). Hamlet's 'songs' to Ophelia promise only to dismay. Moreover their ensuing sexual double-speak belongs to a prince fatally but brilliantly fissured in mind and whose 'antic disposition' as much wears him as he wears it (I.v). It makes for perfect incongruity that on re-sighting the ghost Hamlet vows revenge 'with wings as swift as meditation' (I.v). Delay, or rather its sustained contemplation, indeed becomes its own perverse kind of action.

Shakespeare so positions Hamlet as both his own subject and his own object, the Hamlet who in speaking of his circumstance increasingly construes it as though from outside himself. Horatio may well warn him, on the return of the ghost, of his 'wild and whirling words' (I.v). They will persist, often displaced and ludic yet with a force of logic against any or all apparent illogic. Language in this fashioning becomes its own pre-emptive dynamic as though always more given to speaking Hamlet than he it. Oscar Wilde, the modern for whom fin-de-siècle aestheticism was the touchstone, alights on this point in *De Profundis* with typical brio. He observes of Hamlet:

> The dead have come armed out of the grave to impose on him a mission at once too great and too mean for him. He is a dreamer and he is called upon to act . . . He keeps playing with action, as an artist plays with a theory. He makes himself the spy of his proper actions, and listening to his own words knows them to be but 'words, words, words.' Instead of trying to be the hero of his own history, he seeks to be the spectator of his own tragedy.[15]

Is not this sense of displacement the very foreshadow of the bid to grasp, and yet more to the point, to master alterity as 'modern' condition? Hamlet anticipates human fissure, alienation, as variously explored in the spectrum of European modernism that embraces Kierkegaard, Gogol, Kafka, Camus or Beckett. To these we might add Goya and 'El sueño de razón produce monstruos' ('The dream of reason produces monsters'), another visionary as to how the mind both feeds and yet hexes the inward state of humanity's being.

The self Hamlet 'authors', accordingly, proliferates: procrastinator, melancholic, graveyard philosopher, disenchanted lover, conspirator. The one incarnation, however, in which he fails, or finally approaches in the violent irony of the fight scene (several deaths,

46 MODERNS – CHAUCER TO CONTEMPORARY FICTION

not one), is that of revenger. Rather, at every turn, it is less blade or toxin than utterance that serves as his working insignia. At odds with the world so, also, he is with (and within) himself. As much as that takes the form of interior monologue, or the proliferation of asides, it also in slivers of improvisation involves his frequent savagery of wit.

Unsurprisingly given their density, these quips time and again fail to be readily understood even as they stir question and even pain. 'How pregnant sometimes his replies are' (II.ii) says Polonius. 'I have nothing with this answer' (III.ii) says Ophelia. In exchange with Gertrude over her replacement of his father with Claudius the pivot again is one of word-centredness. To her reprimand 'you answer with an idle tongue' he replies in ironic parallel 'Go, go, you question with a wicked tongue' (III.iv). She will go on to aver, in an echo of how King Hamlet has been poisoned, 'These words like daggers enter in my ears' (III.iv). Each, to whom Claudius, or Rosencrantz and Guildenstern, or even Osric (in the mockery made of him in the references to the weather, V.ii) can be added, respond to Hamlet as though he speaks to them while engaged in an unyielding dialogue of one.

Key moments and exchanges amplify the effect. When he ponders his chance to dispose of Claudius at prayer he holds back, unwilling to allow his uncle the chance of a 'purged' soul in death. Rather his sword, he reasons, should be better wielded with Claudius drunk, or in a rage, or abed with Gertrude. 'This is bait and salary, not revenge' (III.iii) is his rumination. Remorse seizes him at news of Ophelia's death, yet his bitter awareness ('I loved Ophelia' V.i) sounds more like a stunned message to himself than to the Queen and her retinue. His celebrated taunt of Polonius ('very like a whale' III.ii) spills over into sardonic regret that the arras stabbing was of the counsellor and not Claudius ('I took thee for thy better' III.iv). The gloss he gives to having Rosencrantz and Guildenstern executed in the wake of the substituted letter to the King of England resorts unexpectedly to an image of sexual intimacy ('They did make love to this employment' V.ii).

Whether directed ad hominem, or to specific listeners, Hamlet's words increasingly imply their true pitch to be as much for his own contemplative savouring. Soliloquy, or each run of dialogue, rise to their immediate occasion yet at the same time round back on themselves, voice and voice-over. 'To be or not to be', typically, bespeaks

Hamlet under duty of revenge while enlarging to contemplation of death's status in life's being. Caustic snaps of wit like the jibe at the dead Polonius 'at supper' with the worms (IV.iii) give death's head humour to the start and stop of human mortality. The effect, in Kenneth Burke's important formulation, is precisely one of language as symbolic action.[16] It makes not only for how Shakespeare encodes his play's history-narrative but his sense of the 'modern' condition. In these respects we can again invoke William Hazlitt, in his classic essay on *Hamlet*:

> It is *we* who are Hamlet. The play has a prophetic truth, which is above that of history ... He is, as it were, wrapped up in his reflections, and only *thinks aloud*.[17]

It will doubtless risk the arbitrary to offer selective instances of the ways *Hamlet* engages the spectator/reader with the prince as a figure recognisably 'modern', or at the very least, 'proto-modern'. Let three instances do illustrative working duty: the 'mousetrap' dumb-show and its spoken sequel (III.ii); the soliloquy 'How all occasions do inform against me' (IV.iv); and the delivery of Hamlet's intermittent death oration as it arises out of the duel with Laertes (V.ii).

Of these the first gives key reflexive import. Hamlet's instructions to the First Player have long passed into legend, stage speech to be delivered 'trippingly on the tongue' and performance to 'suit the action to the word, the word to the action' (III.ii). In all respects, and drawing upon Shakespeare's dual credential as himself dramatist and actor, the prerequisite has to be 'modesty of nature', neither strut not bellow but 'imitated humanity'. Acting, however, takes on compound implication, the player's performance appositely the index for Hamlet's augmenting outsiderness to himself.

The orchestration of the Gonzaga-Baptista-Lucianus imbroglio, with interval commentary, Hamlet explicitly acknowledges to be aimed at Claudius's 'seeming'. The play-script revised by his own hand serves him as all-to-purpose counterplot, the avowed mousetrap to catch the conscience of the king. Yet the onstage plotters, he reminds, can only 'poison in jest' even though their plot signifies 'a knavish piece of work'. The implications also reach well beyond exposing Claudius's machinations or Gertrude's collusion. For as

48 MODERNS – CHAUCER TO CONTEMPORARY FICTION

the mousetrap teases art's imitation of life, and its reverse, it also speaks directly to Hamlet's own situation.

Literally and figuratively he himself has become author and player, and also chorus, in lieu of taking the 'life' action bequeathed him by his father's murder. In this sustained cross-ply of forms of 'acting' Hamlet is put to examine his very enactment of self, the 'I' given to scrutiny of the 'me'. Implicitly the turnings of 'modern' selfhood, the self given to examination of its own turnings, come visibly, audibly, into consideration.

The process gains confirmatory expression once the players bring in the recorders. Hamlet's speech to Rosencrantz and Guildenstern, full of local wit and joust, gives notice of his suspicion of their willingness to act as agents in Claudius's new plot. More implicitly it silhouettes the larger paradigm of the degree to which any one self can or will permit revelation of true bearings. The terms at work say all. Hamlet uses the music of the recorders as his device to speak of being himself played upon, his 'stops', and yet equally of his resistance to being sounded from 'my lowest note to the top of my compass' (III.iii). He both resists the 'music' meant to catch him out ('you cannot play upon me' III.iii) while, contradictorily, possessed of the discordant 'music' revolving within himself.

These same implications preside in 'How all occasions do inform against me' (IV.iv). Hamlet acknowledges the dragnet of thought ('thinking too precisely on the event') over action ('a father killed, a mother stained, excitements of my reason and my blood'). 'How stand I then' gives the keynote, another in his increments of self-query. It again accords that, having perused his 'dull revenge', the substitution of 'sleep and feed' for 'This thing's to do', he resolves that 'My thoughts be bloody, or be nothing worth!' The choice of 'thoughts' carries situating double-import, whatever the fierceness of resolve to take action also cerebration, the check of introspective mind.

In the final unfolding of events, the combat with Laertes under the regal scheming of Claudius, with Horatio and Osric in attendant witness, Hamlet as much gives face to himself as his fellow duellist (V.ii). His regret at having to sword-fight with Laertes brings commentary as to how he has committed error ('Give me your pardon, sir. I have done you wrong'). In so saying, he also divulges his sense of fissure – 'sore distraction', 'roughly awake', 'madness'. He addresses Laertes from the inside out, the speaker once more auditing his own speech:

> Was't Hamlet wronged Laertes? Never Hamlet.
> If Hamlet from himself be ta'en away.
> And when he's not himself does wrong Laertes,
> Then Hamlet does it not, Hamlet denies it.
> Who does it then? His madness. (V.ii)

The last incarnation lies in the self-obituarist at whose death by chance poison beseeches Horatio to make live the voice he carries into death. Yet 'Report me and my cause aright' (V.ii), from among his final words, actually underlines a Hamlet who eludes all final report. For Hamlet the 'my story' may well find its close in 'the rest is silence' of death. It also, and incontestably, ends in irresolution, the same determining equivocacy as his life.

Modernity lies deep, echoingly, in Hamlet's wells of introspection. At the level of plot line his thinking aloud replaces literal action, the vaunted imperative of revenge. His inwardness, it becomes clear from the outset, carries a far wider semantics, at once existential, philosophic, that has resounded down time, Augustans to Romantics, Moderns to early and late contemporaries. A selective look at the gallery gives confirmation.

In Tom Stoppard's *Rosencrantz and Guildenstern Are Dead* (1966), *Hamlet* becomes meta-theatre, the play playing itself back through Hamlet's inside-out 'fellow students'. Iris Murdoch's *The Black Prince* (1973) has its characters step outside their narrative to supply prologues and epilogues. Ian McEwan's *Nutshell* (2016), its title derived from Hamlet's 'I could be bounded in a nut-shell, and count myself a king of infinite space' (II.ii), re-tells the play as dark-comedy metafiction in the voice of a foetal narrator. However maverick in fashioning, each of these fictions gives recognition to how *Hamlet* sets precedent in the dense mirror-life of the prince. For given their innovatory show and tell, they point up the larger debt: the continuing modernity whereby the mind confronts the plies of its own measure, the challenge of its own dramatic knot.

50   MODERNS – CHAUCER TO CONTEMPORARY FICTION

Notes

1. See, in this connection, Paul A. Cantor, *Hamlet*, Cambridge: Cambridge University Press, 1989, ix: 'Hamlet strikes us as the most modern of Shakespeare's heroes, caught up in a kind of questioning and doubt that seems all-too-familiar in the twentieth century. On the other hand, the story of Hamlet has its roots in the most primitive strata of the imagination, a tale of blood feuds and vengeance, the kind of legend that is found in the fountainhead of many of the great literatures of the west, including Greek and Norse'.
2. Jack Kerouac, *Desolation Angels*, New York: Coward-McCann, 1965. Reprinted New York: Penguin Classics, 2012, 5.
3. Ian McEwan, *Saturday*, London: Jonathan Cape, 2005, 210.
4. Richard Berengarten, *A Portrait in Interviews*, eds Paschalis Nikolaou and John Z. Dillon, Bristol: Shearsman Books, 2017, 97–8.
5. Byron, *Don Juan* (IX–XVI).
6. Erich Auerbach, *Mimesis: The Representation of Reality in Western Literature*, Princeton: Princeton University Press, 1946, 1953, 311.
7. Eric Hoffer, *Truth Imagined*, New York: Harper & Row, 1983, 52.
8. This dimension of Hamlet, actor, self-performer, is given enlightening attention in Peter Conrad, *The Everyman History of English Literature*, London: J. M. Dent & Sons, 1985, 166–8.
9. Morris Dickstein, 'An Outsider in His Own Life', Review of Anthony Cronin, *Samuel Beckett: The Last Modernist*, *New York Times*, 3 August 1997, Section 7, 11.
10. Samuel Johnson, *Preface to Shakespeare*, 1765; *Coleridge's Criticism of Shakespeare: A Selection*, ed. R. A. Foakes, London: Bloomsbury Academic, 1989; T. S. Eliot, 'Hamlet and His Problems', *The Sacred Wood: Essays on Poetry and Criticism*, 1920; Harold Bloom, 'Hamlet', Library of Congress lecture, 2003. For a challenging overview, see Martin Dodsworth, *Hamlet Closely Observed*, London: Athlone Press, 1985.
11. Still relevant in this regard is John Dover Wilson, *What Happens in Hamlet*, Cambridge: Cambridge University Press, 1935.
12. In this respect, see Martin Schofield, *The Ghosts of Hamlet: The Play and Modern Writers*, Cambridge: Cambridge University Press, 1980.
13. Cited in Andrew Jackson, *Elsewhere: Journeys Around Shakespeare's Globe*, London: Bodley Head, 2016.
14. This protean quality in Hamlet, for Salman Rushdie, finds its analogy in the overall form of the play itself. Remembering a conversation with the playwright Howard Benton at Oxford University, he writes, '[Shakespeare] . . . gives us permission to create a work that is many things at once, shape-shifting, a work that doesn't have to be either

a ghost story or love story or a cross-dressing burlesque comedy or a history play or a psychodrama but can be all those things at once, without sacrificing truth or depth or passion or shapeliness or interest, without becoming a confusing, bewildering, shallow, pointless mess.' 'Proteus', *Languages of Truth: Essays 2003–2020*, New York: Random House, 2021, 35–6.

15. Oscar Wilde, 'De Profundis', reprinted in *Complete Works of Oscar Wilde*, London and Glasgow: Collins, 1948, 950.

16. Kenneth Burke, *Language as Symbolic Action: Essays on Life, Literature and Method*, Berkeley: University of California Press, 1966.

17. William Hazlitt, 'Hamlet', *Characters of Shakespeare*, London: Everyman, 1906, 79, 87. For connecting further comment, see Chapter 7, 'Like Nobody But Himself: Modern Hazlitt'.

CHAPTER 4

New Made Idiom: John Donne

Donne, by now, largely gets taken for granted: English poetry's stalwart, its master of metaphysical verse. The assumption, even so, has needed to grow over time, an evolving and sometimes hesitant contour towards 'modern' status. His era, certainly, was not slow to recognise boldness of mind, ingenuity of conceit. Ben Jonson early reports William Drummond as believing 'John Done [sic] the first poet of the World'.[1] Thomas Carew in his 'Elegie upon the Death of the Deane of Paul's, Dr. John Donne' lauds him as the pre-eminent spirit of 'the universal monarchy of wit'.[2] A successor age, however, demurred. Dryden speaks of 'common thoughts in abstruse words'.[3] Pope, given his verse revisions of Donne in the interests of regular scan and caesura, offers 'no imagination but as much wit as I think any writer can have'.[4] Dr Johnson, famous for the indictment of 'heterogeneous ideas . . . yoked by violence together', adds by way of summary allusion to Donne's 'confused magnificence'.[5]

The Romantics, allowing for Coleridge's recognition of 'Wit's forge and fire-blast' and De Quincey's granting of 'extraordinary compass of powers', thought him largely outside their interests.[6] Browning, most notably of the Victorians, took him as predecessor for the dramatic monologue, less the poet of metaphysics than virtuoso of first-person voice. Donne's standing for the Age of Eliot hugely changes the pace, the Renaissance poet but also 'the modern' *avant la lettre*.[7] The case for a pathway from Donne's 'Songs and Sonnets', through to Eliot's 'The Love Song of J. Alfred Prufrock', the Sweeney poems and 'The Waste Land' was made custodially, as though an act of reclamation.

The process more or less dates from *Donne's Poetical Works* (1912) under the editorship of Sir Edward Grierson and its follow-on in his influential anthology *Metaphysical Lyrics and Poems of the Seventeenth Century: Donne to Butler* (1921). Eliot makes the momentousness of Donne explicit in his review-essay of Grierson's

52

anthology for the *Times Literary Supplement* in 1921 ('The Metaphysical Poets'), which he would then include in his *Selected Essays* (1932). 'A thought in Donne was an experience' he observes aphoristically, poetry whose dynamic fusion of thought and feeling he saw as guideline to imagist new poetics.[8] Eliot also supplies a general gloss in relationship to Donne:

> There are two ways in which we may find a poet to be modern: he may have made a statement which is true everywhere and for all time . . . or there may be an accidental relationship between his mind and our own.[9]

Close reading, practical criticism, has gone on to find especial fertility in Donne's verse, a major factor in widening the modernity of his appeal. William Empson in *Seven Types of Ambiguity* (1930) unthreads the intricacy of metaphor in 'A Valediction: Of Weeping.'[10] F. R. Leavis in 'The Line of Wit' celebrates the 'extraordinary force of originality' which makes him 'without being the less felt as of his period, contemporary' (1936).[11] American New Criticism, Cleanth Brooks for example on 'The Canonization' in *The Well Wrought Urn* (1947), could hardly have found more amenable fare for formalist analysis.[12] Interpretation, source scholarship, and editions, notably by Rosemund Tuve, J. B. Leishman, Helen Gardner and A. Alvarez, has much settled upon the poetics in Donne that so drew Eliot.[13] The upshot, for the modernist reader as for the modernist writer, has been Donne still the Elizabethan or Jacobean but also in appeal the perennial immediate. F. O. Matthiessen, writing in the 1930s, was able to fashion a necessary summary:

> The jagged brokenness of Donne's thought has struck a chord in our age, for we have seen a reflection of our own problem in which his passionate mind, unable to find any final truth in which it could rest, became fascinated with the process of thought itself.[14]

Andrews Wanning gives a connecting angle in 1962 when he writes 'the cause of Donne was the cause of modern poetry' with its underlying question of the poetics involved.[15] In this respect Donne's own phrase of 'new found idiom' in from 'A Valediction: of the Booke' comes into relevance. For however positioned in time and place as the writer of love verse, religious sonnet, satire, elegy, anniversary, valedictory or even doctrinal sermon, Donne achieves a compositional temperament congenial to the modern turn. His poetry not only negotiates but enacts the contradictions of desire, the unrest of psyche, the elusive desirability of sustaining generic truth or belief. In this respect his propulsive density of locution takes all before it, well beyond Elizabethan or Jacobean conceit.

Other poets of the age, duly or otherwise designated metaphysical, notably add to the impetus. Andrew Marvell's 'To His Coy Mistress' compels in its theatre of sexual intimacy. George Herbert's 'The Collar' magisterially queries faith and its loss. Richard Crashaw's 'A Hymn to Sainte Teresa' aspires to the devotional sublime. Abraham Cowley's sequence *The Mistress* regulates the dramas of love into the one album. Donne continues to outpace each. His best-known interests play their part. Body and mind submit to love. World and deity engage in riddling counter-pulls. The expanding oceanic atlas beckons. The New Science (which is not to discount interest in what would become pseudo-sciences like astrology and alchemy) engages his intellectual horizons, be it astronomy, Ptolemaic systems of celestial motion, ocular physiology, the evolution of microscopic lenses, or the properties of chemistry and matter.[16] As equally, however, has to be Donne's expressive vitality, precisely the modern of his 'new made idiom'.

T. S. Eliot was not alone in seeing Donne's poetry resources as wholly apposite to the authoring of modernity, just as he and fellow modernists had found themselves drawn to the visionary *symbolisme* of Rimbaud, Verlaine, Laforgue and Valéry with Baudelaire as patron spirit. In Donne was to be met, and heard, a forerunner in the quest for language agile enough to meet not just the divisions of personal desire but of the damaged twentieth century. Eliot's lexicon of 'etherized' patient, 'windy spaces' or 'cruellest month' updates Donne, the modern of English Renaissance best poetry carried echoingly into twentieth-century succession.[17]

What, it can again be asked, makes Donne so especially modern? Erotic or sacred, his poems rarely fail to convey the often tempestuous nexus of engaged life, the press of senses and intellect. The upshot is poetry that at one and the same time issues almost tactile recognition of its own workings. 'I sing not, siren-line, to tempt, for I/ Am harsh' he writes in 'To Mr. S. B.'. Complexity of first-person voice in poetry abundantly has antecedents, the odes of Pindar or Dante, the lyrics of Spenser or Sydney. But Donne manages a fresh degree of charge, unique momentum. It has helped make him sound recognisably modern.

The exhilarating summonses especially count in this respect. 'Come, Madam, come, all my powers defie,/ Until I labour, I in labour lie' in 'Going to Bed' wonderfully emulates exasperated command. 'Goe, and catch a falling starre' in 'Song' prefaces men's search for 'woman true'. The aspiration is to seek, and win, the listener's ear. Petrarch's idealisation of love in 'Laura' and his other poetry gets left behind for Donne's lines embody greater urgency, desire and its threat of remorse taken to the edge. Even the prospect of passage into death, as in 'Divine Reflections' ('This is my playes last scene, here heavens appoint/ My pilgrimages last mile'), speaks in live breath of resistance and submission.

Donne's poems, rightly, have come to be recognised for seeking resolution to fracture and for language brilliantly instant yet corded into a whole. The appeal for a later century's modernism, the search of new life bearings in 'The Waste Land' notably, is not hard to fathom. The influence has been only in part Donne's anatomies of appetite, body and soul. The influence, coevally, has been one of measure, form, persona. If the later modern is to be invoked, that of poets drawing example from Donne, there is every warrant to revisit a selection of even the better-known compositions for markers.

'A Valediction: of the Booke' does not often make the top tier of Donne's poetry. The formulation 'new made idiom' in its third stanza, nonetheless, gives a working latchkey into the presiding manner of his poetry at large. The speaker's request of his lover that she use the letters that have flowed between them to create the record of passion worthy of its enduring 'booke' supplies the conceit. The love in question, given the pair's current separation, is to be rewritten from 'our manuscripts', their 'myriad' letters not just private confirmation of ardour or loyalty but their place in history. The poem not merely reports but imaginatively re-stages the urge to posterity of the love involved. Keats's well-known dictum of a poem's not meaning but being comes to mind.

Given the prospect for the lovers of creating their own exclusive 'booke', the poem envisages latitude elided into longitude, space into time, absence into presence. In consequence, in the speaker's surmise, the reproduced correspondence will compare, imperishably, with the great texts of divinity, or law, or statesmanship. The 'Valediction' to this end stages itself as a 'letter' about prior letters, its farewell in fact a shrewd contradiction of farewell. 'New found idiom' exactly pertains and at the same time carries its reflexive implications for the poem in progress. The one seams, tactically, into the other. In this, and however set as though time-present, it not only looks to time's longer prospect but gives grounds to be thought wholly modern.

Writerly metaphor likewise enters and propels 'The Triple Foole'. How not to recognise the double wink in its opening lines?

> I am two fooles, I know,
> For loving, and for saying so
> in whining Poetry . . .

The poem circles on itself. The vexations or betrayals of love can surely find outlet in nothing other than the act of poetry. As the earth's 'narrow crooked lanes' purge 'fretfull' salt from the oceans, so verse similarly must 'draw my paines'. But such harbours grand illusion, false hope. The poet's 'whine' in the face of love, and to be likened to boundless ocean, does not meet the task. Broken love can never truly be assuaged. The poetry that captures this truth itself can be open to accusation of betrayal: it simply 'fetters' grief. This amounts to 'Rimes vexation', the poem's reminder of hurt.

That the speaker goes un-spared when he hears another's love verse gives him further consternation. But, again, more is involved. Poetry about poetry's inefficacy in the relief of heartbreak stirs added pain. In Donne's paradoxical line the poem he hears 'by delighting many, frees againe/ Griefe'. The poet has so become the triple fool of poet, lover and reader-listener. His cautionary maxim prevails – 'Who are a little wise, the best fooles be'. Befooled lovers make for Donne's theme, but made articulated by his verse's just right 'modern' command.

'The Canonization' long has taken on classic imprimatur. 'For God's sake hold your tongue, and let me love' gives celebrated stride to proceedings along with the injunction to 'chide my palsie, or my gout' or 'my five gray hairs . . . flout'. Rebuke of the inquisitor, friend or otherwise, adds to the speaker's use of the imperative ('Take you a course, get you a place'). Connecting tropes build dynamically. Sea commerce will remain uninjured by this love, land remain un-flooded. Tapers will burn only at the behest of the lovers themselves. Eagle and dove, contrasting avian incarnations of force and mildness, convey the lovers's pairing. The hermaphroditic phoenix can be reborn in them. Donne even daringly imagines his speaker and lover, and their inseparability, to braid into a species of sainthood, the beatific in the secular. A closing stanza envisages the eyes at once 'one another's hermitage' and outward-facing 'mirrors'. These are eyes that gaze true for the lovers while acting also as 'spies' upon the 'Countries, Townes, Courts' of the very world allegedly distanced on account of their hermetic one-to-one devotion.

The poem bears the signature of its time in alluding to 'the Kings reall, or his stamped face', but it also presages time well ahead. The drama of its speaking voice, the compounds and counterflows of image, give just the right impact to the vision of human intimacy being invoked. Donne's headiness of subject matter is held by the poem's assurance of form, the 'well wrought urne' of the last stanza. In consequence, and although 'The Canonization' likely arises out of the historic specifics of Donne's clandestine marriage and downturn in fortune, that far from detains it in the seventeenth century.

In 'The Sunne Rising' Donne's élan again is unmistakable. The opening image of the 'busie old foole' sun to be questioned, indeed chastised, as 'saucy' peeper upon a pair of lovers, shows exquisite calculation. Mock-umbrage feeds the opening question of 'Why does thou . . . call on us?'. The follow-on imperatives mimic dismissal. Chide late schoolboys and sour apprentices opens the list. Summon huntsmen now that the king will ride follows. Order ants to go about their 'harvest offices' reads command. Love, it is to be understood, has prerequisites, desiderata, and needs to be left to its business wholly unfettered. Donne, as it were, knows he is about stage-set.

Would-be braggadocio enters. The speaker's blink can eclipse the sun, but is held back simply to keep the beloved in view even as she 'blinds' those who see her and incarnates the splendour of

Indian spice or regal power. Contradiction, similarly, applies, she 'all States', himself 'nothing is'. Princes can only shadow the pair. Honour must play the mimic. Wealth amounts to mere alchemy. The sun itself lives a half-existence, its happiness partial even as it does duty in warming the earth and the lovers. Heat, brilliance of light, rather, centre in the bed within 'these walls', the epicentre for love-making and lovers's sphere to rival the sun's sphere. To limit Donne to a writer of conceits has always been to fall short. 'The Sunne Rising' drives its principal metaphor hard, love's intensity in time and place as modern as all the ages in which it occurs.

'The good-morrow', the lover's voice intimate, full of query, would meet little difficulty in appealing to a poet of modernist ear and eye. The opening of 'I wonder by my troth, what thou and I/ Did, till we lov'd' hovers at the edge of faux-inquiry. Dream, for once, runs short of reality, the mistress's beauty easily exceeding that of prior 'fancy'. The plait of imagery bears Donne's habitual flair, not least 'waking souls' as against waking bodies after the night's love-making. Love itself becomes a process of dilation as the 'one little roome' transposes into 'an every where'. Other maps supply comparison ('Let sea-discoverers to new worlds have gone'). Why not a 'map' of discovered territory unique to the lovers themselves ('Let us possess one world')? Their faces, in the continuance of geographic metaphor, evolve into 'hemispheares' beyond any North or West.

The poem's 'thou and I' have become so 'alike' that no slackening, no death, can cause un-joining. The 'morrow' in question thereby implies all 'morrows', the permanence of heart. The poem affects mockery of its good faith declarations. How much actual credence to give 'wondering' at any life before the love at hand? How best in the lines that close the poem to understand that 'What ever dyes, was not mixed equally' and so, for speaker and beloved, 'none can die'? Whether designated 'Song' or 'Sonet', 'The good-morrow' takes hold as the perfect witness-poem to love as the presiding one but also perennial moment. However ostensibly a soliloquy, the poem's 'I wonder by my troth', and the injunctions to follow, brilliantly create the participant listener. Modern invitation reads to hand, recognition of shared sensation.

JOHN DONNE 59

'The Will' recapitulates most of these tactics. The speaker's pose of confessant, and giver of apparent last will and testament, elevates the figure of audience to seeming bedside witness. A swerve of voice operates. For this end-of-life farewell in fact is about living, the survival of the lover's heart after the setback of abandonment. No small part of the poem's lament, moreover, derives from the pairing of older woman with the besotted younger lover. Love has made mockery of him in the person of a mistress 'Who thinks her friendship a fit proportion/ For younger lovers'. In this light, he insists, let all be given away, body, mind, belief, achievement, and above all, let there be no further engagement with love itself.

So, ostensibly, runs the thrust of things, Donne's cryptic enumeration of the need to empty the self of anything and all in the wake of repudiated devotion. 'My last gaspe' has eventuated from 'Great love'. The 'some legacies' of the passion that has gone before assume a kind of willed inflation, six stanzas of sublime petulance. The achievement lies in Donne's handling of the younger man's listed outpour, his hyperventilation. The temper is bittersweet, declamatory, and implicitly edited as though to recognise that events now exceed his expressive capacity.

The opening play on 'eyes' gives notice. The lover's once love-blinded eyes must join those of all-seeing Argus, his tongue gifted to Fame, his ears given to ambassadors, his tears to other women or the sea. The list aggregates into a metaphoric anatomy of melancholy, an inventory of body parts under bitter disburdening. Physiology, moreover, is but the one track. Character is another, starting with consignment of 'my contancie' (presumably to his mistress) to 'the planets'. Other proposed discards include giving away truth to the court, ingenuity worthy of the Jesuits, and faith to un-protestant Catholicism. As Donne unfolds them, the speaker's dispiriting experience recalls the 'indignity' of a love made inadequate by his beloved on grounds of 'disparity'.

Nor does the sloughing-off end there. He must give up reputation, effort, sickness, the toll of bell for the dead, books, medals, and wholly of pertinence both 'I in Ryme' and 'mine English tongue'. All can be dispatched to one or another destination. And who to blame? Love. The closing stanza affects to report exhaustion ('I'll give no more'). Love has exerted demand of ransom upon not only heart but mind. In the poem's exaggeration, the lover opts for death that will leave him, his loved one, and love itself, 'annihilated'. This, he says in rueful accusation, 'Thou, Love, taughtst me'. Donne has his poem monitor its very making even as his speaker makes complaint, reflexivity not only successful in effect but once more as modern for any subsequent age as for its own time.

To move to the sacred poetry, and fully in the context of English religious history, in no way diminishes Donne's modernity. Theological expertise has inevitably dwelt upon negotiation of Catholic and Anglican fault line, doctrinal manoeuvring, the obsession with earthly fault and spiritual forgiveness. The wrestles of belief, penitent hope, again avail themselves of idiom 'new-found'. A 'Holy Sonnet' as ingeniously contrarian as 'Death be not proud' ('death, thou shalt die') shares the same prosody with the love poetry. 'A Litanie' ('Heare us, O heare us Lord') reads at one with the voice-theatre of his earlier verse. A supplicant 'hymn' like 'Good Friday, 1613, Riding Westward' ('O think me worth Thine Anger, punish me') draws on pain-pleasure familiar in the travails expressed in the love poetry. 'Modern' Donne in no way lessens across his chosen genres.

Rarely can the continuum be more available than in 'Batter my heart, three person'd God', Sonnet XIV of his 'Divine Meditations'. That the poem has become infinitely well known, another Donne classic, little surprises. Voicing could not be more vigorous, line of paradox more compelling. The sustained trope of ravishment, the appeal to have God seize the soul as though implicated in sexual domination, has its daring. The would-be 'victim', to add to the torque, behaves as readiest supplicant. Interpretation has even evoked de Sade. Seizure or rape turns back on itself albeit for spiritual ends. Donne's vitality understandably arrests, a kind of delicious shock.

One turns to the Donne staples, muscular language, control of measure, resource of metaphor. The opening imperative ('batter my heart'), the prospect of God at the threshold ('knocke, breathe, shine, and seek to mend'), and the prospective 'overthrow' and 'usurpation' of the supplicant, carry far more than religious freight. The issue of quest for divine love ('dearly I love you'), that of the believer spiritually enamoured, consorts with the language of erotic assault. The trope extends into the speaker's notion of himself 'betroth'd' to the world ('your enemie') and his need for earthly divorce into the liberating imprisonment of God's domain. The final spiritual-sexual plait tilts even more headily towards belief as invitation to seizure ('never shall be free,/ Nor ever chast, except you ravish me'). This enactive flair carries all before it. Donne's modernity, whether the divine or secular poems, remains in how his 'new found idiom' gives full imaginative carriage to his directions of vision.

Donne as modern, or pre-modern, assuredly does not disconnect him from his Elizabethan or Jacobean moorings. For in common with Shakespeare, near-contemporary, he arises from his own era, but under modernism's taste for him enlarges our sense of that era. However time-specific, the well-born gallant, European traveller and soldier, and Dean of St Paul's caught between flesh and spirit, apostasy and right belief, incontrovertibly he has become the greater fusion. Who, now, does not imagine they hear themselves in his work? 'A Valediction: of the Book', in 'new made idiom' as in conception, typically manages the inter-muscle of sensation and thought. To that end it serves coevally to mark both the Elizabethan modern and later modern of Donne's poetry.

Notes

1. Ben Jonson, *Conversations with William Drummond of Hawthornden*. First published, 1833.
2. Thomas Carew, 'An Elegie upon the Death of the Deane of St Paul's, Dr John Donne', *Poems*, 1633.
3. John Dryden, 'An Essay on Dramatick Poesie', 1688.
4. Alexander Pope, *Poems*, 1735.
5. Samuel Johnson, 'The Life of Cowley', *The Lives of the Poets*, 1779–81.
6. *The Notebooks of Samuel Taylor Coleridge*, ed. Kathleen Coburn, Princeton, NJ: Princeton University Press, 1957–61; 'Notes on the Poems of Donne', Thomas de Quincey, 'Rhetoric' (1828), reprinted in *Works*, Vol. X, 40, Edinburgh: Thomas Hogg, 1853–60.
7. For a fuller account, see Helen Gardner, 'Introduction', *John Donne: A Collection of Critical Essays*, Englewood Cliffs, NJ: Prentice Hall. Inc., 1962, 1–12.
8. T. S. Eliot, *Selected Essays*, London: Faber & Faber, 1932, 247.
9. T. S. Eliot, 'John Donne', *The Nation and Athenaeum*, xxxiii, 1923, 331. See also A. Alvarez, *The School of Donne*, London: Chatto & Windus, 1961, 13.

62   MODERNS – CHAUCER TO CONTEMPORARY FICTION

10. William Empson, *Seven Types of Ambiguity*, London: Chatto & Windus, 1930, Chapter IV. Reprinted London: Penguin/Peregrine Books, 1961, 139–45.

11. F. R. Leavis, 'The Line of Wit', *Revaluation*, London: Chatto & Windus, 1936. Reprinted London: Penguin/Peregrine Books, 1964, 18.

12. Cleanth Brooks, *The Well Wrought Urn*, New York: Harcourt Brace & World, 1947.

13. Rosamund Tuve, *Elizabethan and Metaphysical Imagery*, Chicago: University of Chicago Press, 1947; J. B. Leishman, *The Monarch of Wit: An Analytical and Comparative Study of the Poetry of John Donne*, London: Hutchinson, 1951; Helen Gardner (ed.), *The Metaphysical Poets*, London: Penguin, 1957; and A. Alvarez, *The School of Donne*, London: Chatto & Windus, 1961.

14. F. O. Matthiessen, *The Achievement of T. S. Eliot*, New York: Oxford University Press, 1935.

15. Andrews Wanning, Introduction, *Donne: The Laurel Poetry Series*, New York: Dell Publishing, 1962, 10.

16. In this respect, see vintage studies like Charles Coffin, *John Donne and the New Philosophy*, New York Columbia University Press, 1937, and Marjorie Hope Nicholson, *The Breaking of the Circle: Studies in the Effect of the 'New Science' upon Seventeenth Century Poetry*, Evanston, IL: Northwestern University Press, 1950.

17. These well-known phrasings, respectively, are taken from 'The Love Song of J. Alfred Prufrock', 'Gerontion' and 'The Waste Land'.

CHAPTER 5

A Good Quantity of Heterogeneous Material: Laurence Sterne

'Deliberate fantasticality': George Saintsbury's phrase in his Introduction to the 1912 Everyman edition of *Tristram Shandy* (1761–7) allows for both detractors and adherents.[1] On the one hand writers from Dr Johnson ('odd'), to Goldsmith ('obscene'), to Thackeray ('worn out old scamp'), have given Sterne the back of their hand.[2] A century on, F. R. Leavis's notorious dismissal of the novel as 'irresponsible (and nasty) trifling' adds to the disaffection.[3] The counter view places the novel at infinitely higher altitude. Boswell speaks of a 'damned clever book'. Nietzsche lauds Sterne as 'the supplest of authors'. Virginia Woolf in her Introduction to *A Sentimental Journey Through France and Italy* (1768), the successor to *Tristram Shandy*, applauds 'the gap this astonishingly agile pen has cut in the dense thick-set hedge of English prose'.[4] One can add Gogol, Balzac and Kundera among co-admirers. Flawed or triumphant, the novel refuses to lie quiet.

Sterne's early readers, whether or not they thought he had used his powers of invention to ill-result, were clear about one facet. *Tristram Shandy* belonged in the tradition of 'learned wit'.[5] Sterne little hesitates to display his repertoire of Greek and Latin authorship whether Menippus, Aristotle, Longinus, Cicero or Horace. His philosophic affinity with the John Locke he calls 'sagacious' recurs, especially the insistence on experience over abstract idea in *Essay on Human Understanding* (I-13). He invokes Erasmus with regularity, and albeit to ironic ends, Sorbonne theological and legal authority in the matter of excommunication. Literary debts win repeated acknowledgement, Rabelais, Cervantes or Montaigne, with hurrahs for the satire of Dryden and Swift (notably *A Tale of a Tub*).

In turn *Tristram Shandy* itself has become the precursor. Salman Rushdie opens *Midnight's Children* (1981) with his intertextual

63

64   MODERNS – CHAUCER TO CONTEMPORARY FICTION

loan of Mr Shandy and the monthly winding of the clock. Alexander
Theroux in *Darconville's Cat* (1981) readily cites Sterne as a fore-
runner in sleight of voice. Machado de Assis writes his Sternean-
Brazilian memorial fake-marriage classic *Dom Casmurro* (1899) and
Juan Goytisolo his fantasia of upended Spain in *Count Julian* (1970).
Shandyism, only slightly less than surrealism, magic realism or, lat-
terly, the cut-up, joins them in having become an *-ism*.[6]

The novel begins as it continues, the author pledged in the voice
of Tristram to the ludic highs and lows of the Shandy dynastic round
while keeping up guard in anticipation of query or hostile critique.
Like the fictions for which Sterne has been an influence, *Tristram
Shandy* challenges any inclination to leisured passivity, ever the
embattled text, ever fists raised authorship. To which purpose Sterne
has Tristram mock-intervene in the story with asides, commentary,
supposed throat-clearings, the conscious invitation to writer–reader
duet. The vaunt, the reflexivity, of his novel insistently distances it
from the 'objective' third person fiction of Fielding or Richardson,
Defoe or Smollett – which is not to deny that they, too, in various
degrees, intervene to comment on their own storytelling. Put otherwise, Sterne writes in divergence from, perhaps even in considerable
opposition to, D. H. Lawrence's prescription of trusting the tale not
the teller or, as in this case, the ostensible teller.

Whether seemingly *in propria persona*, or through the agency
of Tristram, Sterne could hardly be readier with annotation of his
novel's generative processes even as it delivers their upshot. The
challenge he sets himself, Tristram as his surrogate, is to subvert any
and all illusion of some one straight line or fixity to human behaviour and assuredly of its literary narrative. The process, throughout *Tristram Shandy*, takes the notion of unreliable narrator to the
edge. Tristram makes repeated, and invariably playful, confession
as to his supposed authorial fallibility. The outcome yields a version of *la comédie humaine* both at eye level and ear to the ground,
'hobby-horse' eccentricity yet also the domestic quotidian.

Perhaps unsurprisingly, given the novel's gamesomeness, *Tristram
Shandy* has won plaudits for how it gels with signature literary modernity (and postmodernity). These point to fictions by, and beyond, say,
Joyce or Woolf. Borges's *Ficciones* (1944), with their miniatures of
labyrinth and chance, signifies one footfall. Beckett novels like *Mal-
loy* (1951), with its double-column voices, makes for resemblance.
B. S. Johnson's *The Unfortunates* (1967) as improvisatory box-novel

takes a major cue from Sterne. In his near irreal pen-and-ink illustrations for an early edition of *Tristram Shandy* William Hogarth saw in advance and as well as most Sterne's gyrations at work. For a far later age Don DeLillo in *White Noise* (1985) offers a fortuitous bearing as to Sterne's powers of serious play in the observation 'The world is full of abandoned meanings'.[7]

Parenthesis, digression, contra-flow, contingency, time-shifts of clock and consciousness, Sterne insists, shape the way we comport ourselves. Why not transpose and fold them into the literary page, an early variety as it were of narrative superscript? Why not acknowledge the very materiality of the book, its physical bookness, in equal part with its styling of page-for-page story? Why not a book that ends with its declared un-ending? No writer of Sterne's time takes on these interrogations more gymnastically. The 'modern' of *Tristram Shandy* holds there, or one has grounds to think, thereabouts.

Shandy, etymology reveals, and as Sterne would have known from his family and parish residences in Yorkshire's Halifax, Sutton-on-the Forest and Coxwold, affords local slang for odd, cracked. Getting to Tristram's actual birth, then arriving at his ironically Latinised misname, not to say having his nose flattened by Dr Slop's forceps ('the era of my begetting' I-XXI), and the colloquia and hobby-horsing of father and uncle, put the novel into a kind of lively enactive delay. This mode of narrative gathers force once Corporal Trim, Parson Yorick, the Widow Wadman, and the further Shandy household of Mrs Shandy, the lost son Bobby, and the servants Obadiah and Susannah, are brought into the assemblage. 'This whimsical theatre of ours . . . the SHANDY FAMILY' runs Tristram's fond if rueful designation (III-XXXIV). Well he might so call it, for contrariety rules the *mise-en-scène* of *Tristram Shandy* and the 'Life and Opinions' on offer.

Guidances to this end are frequent and telling. 'But this bye the bye' (I-XIII) reads an early aside, the promissory note of things to come. 'Bear with me . . . and let me go on, and tell my story my way' (I-XV) Tristram adds by way of follow-on. '*Vive la Bagatelle*' he says of his father's 'notions' (I-XI), phrasing that again carries more than a hint of the larger story being constructed. Embroiled in why Mr Shandy's son should not be to be baptised under 'Papist'

66   MODERNS – CHAUCER TO CONTEMPORARY FICTION

rite, Sterne has Tristram assume equal rank with himself and enjoin the reader he designates 'Madam' to 'get to the next full stop, and read the whole chapter over again' (I-XX). Textuality intrudes and co-exists with text, the storytelling always in acknowledged measure also the story.

Uncle Toby, veteran of Namur and his other continental military campaigns, is duly characterised for the model battlegrounds he builds on his bowling green as 'full of HOBBY-HORSICAL matter' (I-XXIV). Hobby-horses virtually possess the novel. The compendium, alongside fortresses, extends to hearthside fires, pipes, parlour hinges, chambermaids, stairway conversations, whiskers, knots, wigs, buttonholes, breeches, maypoles, habits of thought, chance, medical briefcases, errands, slight incidents, and Paris streets and other travels beyond England. HOBBY-HORSICAL, in other words, stands in for the novel overall. Sterne guys, fondly, not only the Shandy world and the niches of its lived-in people ('so Cervantic a cast' IV-XXXIII), but the novel's custodianship of that world (Tristram can imagine himself a 'Sancho Panza' IV-XXXII).

As the plot line evolves through Walter's pipe-smoking discourses, Toby's fortifications, Trim's sergeantry, Slop's medical clumsiness, Yorick's sermons or the Widow Wadman's coquettishness, together with Tristram's prospective education at the hands of his Shandy kin, so they come wound in contextual digressions often enough themselves the subject of digressions:

> Digressions, incontestably, are the sunshine: – they are the life, the soul, of reading; – take them out of this book, for instance, – you might as well take the book along with them; – one cold eternal winter would reign in every page of it; restore them to the writer, – he steps forth like a bridegroom, – bids All Hail, brings in variety, and forbids the appetite to fail. (I-XXII)

Whether Sterne is indeed to be thought having positioned himself over Tristram's shoulder, the aim of his paragraph is emphatic. The storytelling's every show of digression, each thread, spiral, torque, analogy, graphic or even gap, for all that it looks random, acts in the interest of the one concert. Sterne, let it be said, and in modern spirit and expression, knows what he is doing.

At another early point in the novel, and as though bravura on Tristram's part, notice is offered of the novel's pending gait, the ever more frequent 'stoppages'. The tone mimics confiding word to the reader, the punctuating dashes all to purpose for the fare ahead:

> These stoppages, which I had no conception of when I first set out, – but which, I am convinced now, will increase rather than diminish as I advance, – have struck out a hint which I am resolved to follow, – and that is not to be in a hurry, – but to go on leisurely, writing and publishing two volumes of my life every year; – which, if I am suffered to go on quietly, and can make a tolerable bargain with my bookseller, I shall continue to do as long as I live. (I-XIV)

Joyce would assert that all he required for *Ulysses* was that his reader recognise a work ever to accorded perennial, endlessly attentive, re-reading. Sterne, in his measure ('two volumes of my life every year . . . as long as I live'), looks to be the putative forerunner.

A comparable interjection follows several chapters later, the emphasis again on the novel as contracted with the reader:

> Writing, when properly managed (as you may be sure I think mine is), is but a different name for conversation: As no one who knows what he is about in good company would venture to talk all, – so no author who understands the just boundaries of decorum and good breeding would presume to think all: The truest respect which you can pay to the reader's understanding is to halve the matter amicably, and leave him something to imagine, in his turn, as well as yourself. (II-XI).

Under cover of good manners Sterne seemingly gives notice of authorly invitation. The reader must meet the author's offer halfway, Tristram's fellow conversationalist. Conversation makes for yet another watchword for the novel's currents of stop and start, the one participant voice in exchange with or even talking across its recipient.

Walter Shandy's 'transverse zigzaggery' (III-III), as his hearthside expiations are labelled, along with Toby's 'cross reckonings' (VII-VI), supply more labels for the narration at large. E. M. Forster's notion of Sterne's 'charmed stagnation' looks curiously discrepant in the face of the novel's almost prodigious textual energy.[8] When, for instance, *Tristram Shandy* situates the Author's Preface plumb amid one of the constituent volumes (III-XX), the charge could go up of mere caper, tomfoolery. In fact, as Tristram ponders the balance of wit and judgement, the insistence that the writer address the world's plenty in its every vigour as against elitist 'set dissertations', he rightly bills himself 'no caressing prefacer' (III-XX).

The Preface, its positioning and thrust, offers a symptomatic instance of simulating the very thing it professes. Offered as Shandy father and uncle round out their exchange on 'TIME AND ETERNITY' (III-IX), as Dr Slop attends upstairs with Mrs Shandy and the midwife, and as Corporal Trim repurposes jackboots into mortars for 'the siege of Messina next summer', Sterne has Tristram pause as though taking time to regroup ("tis the first time I have had a moment to spare, – and I'll make use of it and write my preface' III-XX). He follows this with banner irony in speaking of 'books of strict morality and close reasoning such as this I am engaged in' (III-XXXI). Textuality, Sterne's monitoring of his work once more through Tristram, again enters and encloses text. 'Anti-Shandeans', he nudges, may object. If that be the case, then, with bravura as wholly deliberate as purposive, so be it.

Serious or comic zigzaggery, or the unflagging plait of both, *Tristram Shandy* makes clear that there can be few holds barred. Toby's groin wound prompts both sympathy and furtive humour. Tristram's sash-window circumcision parodies male genital surgery. The fanciful and endlessly intruded upon nun-and-nose story of 'Hafen Slawkenbergius Tale' (III-XXXIX) is told as though it were European fabliau. None of these give grounds for thinking Sterne does not have a full and firm grip on his novel's trajectory. To the contrary. The voice-overs indicate Tristram as narrator to be on shared footing with himself as narratee.

Gestures of frustration, even apparent complaint, read as though to mock the controlling hand:

> ... in good truth, when a man is telling a story in the strange way I do mine, he is obliged continually to be going backwards and forwards to keep all tight together in the reader's fancy – which,

LAURENCE STERNE

69

for my part, if I did not take heed to do more than at first, there is
so much unfixed and equivocal matter starting up, with so many
breaks and gaps in it, – and so little service do the stars afford
which, nevertheless, I hang up in some of the darkest passages,
that the world is apt to lose its way, with all the lights of the sun
itself at noonday can give it – and now, you see, I am lost myself!
(VI-XXXIII)

The posture of the fictional author caught out by his authoring solicits reader awareness of the project in play and at the same time issues
a summons to complicity. Sterne's storytelling is that of supervised
indirection. The reader is duly put on notice. Literary-critical modernity, for Roland Barthes, Wolfgang Iser or Stanley Fish, has required
familiarity with theories of reader response, *Rezeptionsästhetik*. Yet
on the basis of *Tristram Shandy* the grounds again suggest Sterne to
have run ahead of the curve. However much a latter-day truism that
writing creates its reader, or that the reader in turn 'creates' the writing, the process has its foreshadow in Sterne's novel.

He duly has much to say about readership, the first-time reader,
the repeat reader, the mis-remembering reader. Any 'dear reader'
convention so only flatters to deceive. Sterne/Tristram names a
plurality of readerships from the vocative opening of 'Madam',
through to 'Sir Critic', 'Your Worships', 'Worships and Reverences',
'Your Ladyships' and 'Your Connoisseurships', and to the epony-
mous 'Janet'. Volubility in the reader coalesces with volubility in
the text, the latter for its interventions, in-text commentaries and
word-and-typography inserts.

'Stay – I have a small account to settle with the reader! . . . It shall
be done in two minutes' (V-VIII) intervenes Tristram midstream as
Trim delivers his impromptu obituary on the dead son Bobby and
on death in general. In exasperation at fatuous as against authentic
scholarship (in this case on water-drinking), Tristram gives himself
to outburst with 'For my part, I am resolved never to read any book
but my own, as long as I live' (VIII-V). The reader, of the eighteenth
or any subsequent century, has cause to recognise Tristram as both
writer and reader, each the one custodially tracking the other.

As to Tristram in his role of writer, Sterne does not hesitate to
offer guidelines. His own discussion, appositely, of 'all nice and
ticklish discussions' has Tristram affect the author pitched *en pleine*

bouche and yet aware of the need for 'discretion' which he glosses as 'fasting':

> Now, when I write full, – I write as if I was never to write fasting again as long as I live . . . In a word, my pen takes its course: and I write as much from the fullness of my heart, as my stomach – . . . But when I indict fasting . . . I pay the world all possible attention and respect . . . and have as great a share of that understanding virtue of discretion as the best of you. – So that betwixt both, I write a careless kind of civil nonsensical, good humoured Shandean book, which will do all your hearts good – And all your heads, too, – provided you understand it. (VI-XVII)

Full and yet discreet, heart and yet head, 'Shandean book' and yet the reader who will 'understand': the passage approaches reflexive manifesto ('my pen takes its course').

One can add for continuation the title phrase of the current chapter taken from Volume IX ('a good deal of heterogeneous matter' IX-XII). In the sexual horseplay of Toby's groin, and the romance charade with the Widow Wadman, Tristram affects to feign unusual reticence in filling out the implications. Appearing the soul of sexual discretion, the appeal he makes once more plays into the pretence of put-upon author ('Now give me all the help you can' IX-XX). Two chapters later he testifies 'We live in a world beset on all sides with mysteries and riddles' (IX-XXII) as though to license the disjunctures of his narrative.

Sterne's modernity resides in this trepidation of open text. The riffs, each 'bye-the-bye', contrarily tether the narrative movement as much as they disperse its energies. Digressions take on pattern. Staggered or dash-laden paragraphs assume inner coherence of meaning. For those of willing eye and ear, the literary entrepreneurship seeks to engage as it challenges, careful to indicate the rationale behind the textual venturing.

Visuals contribute similarly. Pages variously blank, part-filled or wholly blacked-out help encode a novel giving literal show of its actuation. The insertion of a 'marbled' black and white graphic swirl acts as 'the motley emblem of my work!' (III-XXXVI). The contrast of viewable squiggle with 'tolerable straight line' for 'Toby's story,

LAURENCE STERNE

and my own' (VI-XL) and Trim's curvilinear diagram of 'liberty' (IX-IV), offered as the flourish of a stick to indicate Toby's risk of impending loss of celibacy, apply wholly to the novel at large.

Tristram Shandy, perceptibly more than *A Sentimental Journey*, has met with un-slowing tides of scholarship. The comic in Sterne wins repeated focus. 'Everything in this world', he has Tristram cite his father, 'is big with jest – and has wit in it, and instruction too' (V-XXXII).[9] Sterne's classicism fills footnotes. Critics given over to dialogic theory position the book as out-bordering the linear realism of most of his generation's fiction.[10] Judgement, even so, little settles. *Tristram Shandy* veers between scholar-intelligent comic satire or droll jackanapes. On occasion, criticism hedges its bets, the novel the overlap of both. Whichever the inclination Sterne persists, the conjuror and the irrepressible curator, in his novel's resolve upon forging a unique species of modern.

Notes

1. George Saintsbury, 'Introduction', *Laurence Sterne. The Life & Opinions of Tristram Shandy, Gentleman*, London: J. M. Dent, Everyman Library, ix.
2. Most of these estimates are to be found in Alan B. Howes (ed.), *Sterne: The Critical Heritage*, London: Routledge & Kegan Paul, 1971. Revised as *Laurence Sterne: The Critical Heritage*, London and Boston: Routledge & Kegan Paul, 1974. Textual citations throughout are to Volumes I–VIII and relevant chapter. The title phrase appears through IX–XII.
3. F. R. Leavis, *The Great Tradition*, London: Chatto & Windus, 1948, 2, Note 2.
4. Virginia Woolf, 'Introduction', *A Sentimental Journey Through France and Italy*, London: Oxford University Press, 1928, vi.
5. For a definitive account, see D. W. Jefferson, '*Tristram Shandy* and the Tradition of Learned Wit', *Essays in Criticism*, 1, 1951.
6. See, in this respect, Peter Conrad, *Shandyism: The Character of Romantic Irony*, Oxford: Blackwell, 1978.
7. Don DeLillo, *White Noise*, New York: Penguin, 1985, 184.
8. E. M. Forster, *Aspects of the Novel*, London: Edward Arnold, 1927, 146.
9. The following especially apply: Richard Lanham, '*Tristram Shandy*': *The Games of Pleasure*, Berkeley: The University of California Press, 1973; J. M. Stedmond, *The Comic Art of Laurence Sterne: Convention and Innovation in 'Tristram Shandy' and 'A Sentimental Journey'*, Toronto:

72   MODERNS – CHAUCER TO CONTEMPORARY FICTION

University of Toronto Press, 1967; Stuart M. Tave, *The Amiable Humorist: A Study in the Comic Theory and Criticism of the Eighteenth and Nineteenth Century*, Chicago: University of Chicago Press, 1960; and Rufus D. S. Putney, 'Laurence Sterne: Apostle of Laughter', *The Age of Johnson: Essays Presented to Chauncey Brewster*, New Haven, CT: Yale University Press, 1949, 159–70.

10. See, respectively, John Mullan, 'Laurence Sterne and the "Sociality" of the Novel', in *Sentiment and Sociability: The Language of Feeling in the Eighteenth Century*, New York: Oxford University Press, 1988; John Traugott, *Tristram Shandy's World: Sterne's Philosophical Rhetoric*, Berkeley: University of California Press, 1954; Robert Alter, *Partial Magic: The Novel as Self-Conscious Genre*, Berkeley: University of California Press, 1974; Mark Loveridge, *Laurence Sterne and the Argument About Design*, London: Macmillan, 1982; and David Pierce and Jan de Voogd (eds), *Laurence Sterne in Modernism and Postmodernism*, Amsterdam and Atlanta: Rodopi, 1996.

CHAPTER 6

Era's Modern: Byron, Mary Wollstonecraft Shelley, Peacock

Byron has long passed into myth as Regency poet-aristocrat. Mary Wollstonecraft, at still not twenty years of age, wins place as precocious gothic novelist. Thomas Love Peacock, onetime East India Company employee, finds reputation as observer wit. Each in name achieves ranking in English literary history, although rarely for their grasp of what, in their era, might be called their modern times. Byron's *Childe Harold's Pilgrimage* (1812–18) and *Don Juan* (1819–24) evolve not only the hero-adventurer, but do so with the author's identifying roll of manner. Mary Shelley's *Frankenstein; or, the Modern Prometheus* (1818, revised 1831) addresses human darkness, less obstetric melodrama than a fable of ideas. Thomas Love Peacock's *Nightmare Abbey* (1818), regularly shelved as caricature much at the expense of the magisterial figure of Samuel Taylor Coleridge and with strikes at Byron and Shelley, gives fresh figuring to 'conversation' fiction. All three writers, and their work, do not escape cavils. But they share the will to break ground, to establish their own kinds of modern. 'No story is the same to us after a lapse of time; or rather we who read it are no longer the same interpreters' attests George Eliot in *Adam Bede* (1859).

Byron, avowedly English poetry's second generation Romantic with Shelley and Keats, embodies the legend of aristocratic renegade, dead aged twenty-six at Missolonghi, the intending revolutionary in the cause of Greek independence (1821–9) from the Ottoman Empire. That and the best-known poems acknowledged, he has to a degree lessened in popularity. Mary Shelley, heir to Godwin radicalism and Wollstonecraft feminism, eloper and wife with Percy Bysshe Shelley, assumes front place in the halls of literary shock-horror. Less frequently does her best-known work win full heed for ideas as to formation of human identity, the philosophy of being.

73

Peacock, whatever his satiric flair, still tends to exist at the margins, the diverting bit-player. Better regard, allowing for the pastiche, sees anticipation of Dickens, consequential wit. Beyond these kilters in estimation, and the fortuitous overlap of chronology of the principal works, each author invites a quite further layer of recognition. Their writing, to immediate purpose, apportions respective styles of the modern to the arriving century.[1]

Byron inhabits a number of paradoxes. The flamboyance of his life ('Mad, bad and dangerous to know' in Lady Hamilton's heady accolade) competes with his early reputation as poet ('the greatest talent of the century' for Goethe). His modernity, as it struck contemporaries, far from eliminated his sense of continuity from prior literary regimes. Bracing, a next generation, he shows undiluted regard for predecessors. Greek and Latin touchstones recur. Petrarch, Dante, Cervantes, Voltaire, Rousseau make entrances. In English tradition Shakespeare, Milton, Dryden and Swift are each accorded highest place. Pope wins repeated esteem, satire, couplet and caesura held in commanding balance. Walpole, Radcliffe, Beckford fortify his interest in the allures of gothic. Spenser's hereditary *ottava rima* houses the cantos of *Childe Harold* and *Don Juan*. Byron takes on bardic posture of his resolutely individual making but never without undisguised sense of literary heritage.[2]

Issues have centred on the Byronic type, the noble-exilic outsider variously created in poems like 'Manfred' (1817) and 'Cain' (1821), or in the satires launched with *English Bards and Scotch Reviewers* (1809) and to be met in lighter efforts like 'Beppo: A Venetian Story' (1818). His capacity for unsparing coruscation is born out in 'The Vision of Judgment' (1822) with its attack on Robert Southey, whose turn to establishment patronage as Poet Laureate appalled him. Across the oeuvre, however, it has been *Don Juan*, with lesser accompaniment in *Childe Harold*, that emerges as best-known hallmark. There, in appetite and energy, he has his lasting claim to the modern.

Read in contrast with the contemplative tradition of Goldsmith, Gray, Cooper and Collins, or the stately autobiography of Wordsworth's *The Prelude*, *Childe Harold* and *Don Juan* exude Byron's flair for the colloquial. The highly affecting openness, the performative show, not only resist but break through fixed-line stanza and

BYRON, MARY WOLLSTONECRAFT SHELLEY, PEACOCK   75

rhyme. By the time he had *Don Juan* fully in progress Byron knew his poetry's forte. He would reflect modernity as dynamic, cultural change and flux, with the canto boldly adapted as vehicle.[3]

Childe Harold has never had the best of it. Harold veers towards shadow, despite the journeying, the reprobate past, the melancholy, and the determination to escape ennui ('Strange pangs would flash along Childe Harold's brow' I-VIII). The remorse can quickly wear for the reader ('With pleasure drugg'd, he almost longed for woe' I-VI). Narrator and Harold awkwardly get each lost in the other ('But where is Harold?' I-XVI). Lines like 'Self-exiled Harold wanders forth again' (III-XVI) betray near indifference to sequence. Opportunistically other poems enter. 'Adieu' and the lament 'To Inez' appear in Canto I. 'Tambourgi! Tambourgi!'(Canto II) carries battlefield memory. 'Drachenfels' (Canto III) introduces his Rhine-song. The frequency of medievalisms runs the risk of irritation ('Hight', I, III, 'Hark!', I, XXXVIII, 'Lo!', XXXIX, 'Fytte', I, XCIII). *Childe Harold*, on general estimation, always promised more than it delivers.

If *Don Juan* emerges as the stronger *composition*, it nevertheless does disservice to think of *Childe Harold* only through deficits. Topography signifies ('New shores descried make every bosom gay' I-XIV). Lisbon, and the Tagus, Cintra mountains and the Bay of Biscay, possess portside beauty ('Her image floating on that noble tide' I-XVI). Spain is portrayed to fuse soil and the air of adventure ('lovely . . . renown'd, romantic land!' I-XXXV). Brussels becomes 'revelry by nights' (III-XXI). Greece is seen as past civilisation and war-ground, high art and relic, the ambiguity of a 'consecrated land' (II-XCII). Italy's cities, decay duly noted, give rise to admiration ('Fair Florence' II-XXXII, 'Rome . . . city of the soul!' IV-LXXVIII). River, hilltop, forest supply sight and sound in the poet's gaze across Rhine, Lake Leman, The Jura and Albania. This presentation of vista, together with the better soliloquising, anticipate the modern to be met in *Don Juan*.

Don Juan is well known to open with a brandish ('I write this reeling, Having got drunk exceedingly today' I, *Fragment*). Southey, convert to the establishment, becomes 'Epic Renegade' (I-I). Coleridge, teasingly, is enjoined to 'explain his Explanation' (I-II). Wordsworth's 'The Excursion', in length and diction, ill-qualifies as poetry. Byron's own poem, by contrast, he bills maybe self-ironically as 'grand poetic riddle' (VIII-CXXXIX), 'versified Aurora Borealis'

76   MODERNS – CHAUCER TO CONTEMPORARY FICTION

(VII-II), 'nondescript and ever-varying rhyme' (VII-II) and 'my speculation' (XII-XXI). The zest persists, the professed spread of interests ('I write the world' XV-LX), the equally professed confidence
of stride ('I rattle on exactly as I'd talk' XV-XIX). Don Juan as title
figure ('our ancient friend' I-I) is to be rewritten, less the libertine
of 'the labyrinths of love' (VI-XXIII) than the holder-back 'more
seductive,/ Because he ne'er seemed anxious to seduce' (XV-XII).

'Riddle', 'rhyme', 'the world', 'talk', point up the tenor of *Don
Juan*. They indicate historical step-change in the voicing of verse-
narrative. At the outset Byron, or his speaker, gives notice of working
prospectus:

> There's only one slight difference between
> Me and my epic brethren gone before,
> And here the advantage is my own, I ween
> (Not that I have not several merits more,
> But this will more particularly be seen);
> They so embellish, that 'tis quite a bore
> Their labyrinth of fables to thread through,
> Whereas this story's actually true. (I-CCII)

This breezy insouciance pervades *Don Juan*. 'Actually true' story
equivocates, a show of false authentication. Readers from Regency
to recent times have reason to think themselves virtually under
modern command to pay attention.

The poem's sixteen cantos show little drop in spiritedness. Each
love adventure comes glossed with insider speculation on the competing ways of Eros, together with gestures of outright ribaldry. Juan,
although intermittently off-stage, serves as inexhaustibly drawn to
different sight and sound. His love interests become mosaic, successively the beauteous Andalucian Julia, Greek island Haidée,
Sultana Gulbeyaz, the harem's Dudú, together with Catherine of
Russia, Lady Adeline Amundeville and the impassive Aurora. He
transposes into the female-coutured 'Juanna' at the Turkish court,
Byron's playful harem transvestism. The siege of Ismail permits
thoughts on arms and the man, Homer to Napoleon, war's front-
line brutality with the adopted girl-child Leila as survivor icon. The
English scenes, with Juan under Russian ambassadorial credential,
have Byron casting informed eye on money and caste, the rake and
coquette rituals of London and stately home society. Pilgrim's progress, as it has been called, covers a wide menu, private and public.

The poem's ebullience in *Don Juan* out-reaches formality of octet or end-rhyme or even the epic. The pointers to different histories, the remembrance of classic art and sculpture, the political musings, demonstrate forager appetite. Asides of satiric or quasi-philosophical commentary balance latitude of event. Typically Juan is early accredited with 'the arts of riding, fencing, gunnery,/ And how to scale a fortress – or a nunnery' (I-XXXVIII). Equally typical has to be the purported exasperation in capturing the Juan–Julia liaison ('I can't go on;/ I'm almost sorry that I e're begun' I-CXV). The poet Byron so monitors its own creation. The one text – buoyantly – co-exists inside the other. Little wonder *Don Juan* has become his best-known calling-card.

The double thrust, teller of his own equal tale, Byron handles to great advantage. The Haidée episode, full of Rousseauesque echo, closes on his role as author ('laying down my pen, I make my bow' II-CCXVI). In the follow-on to the Ismail battle scenes with Johnson, Juan's fellow English prisoner, the narration avows 'Without, or with, offence to friends or foes,/ I sketch your world exactly as it goes' (VIII-LXXXIX). Summary, to meet the width of board, does not go wanting:

> Reader! I have kept my word, – at least so far.
> As the first canto promised. You have now
> Had sketches of love, temper, travel, war –
> All very accurate, you must allow,
> And *epic*, if plain truth should prove no bar:
> For I have drawn much less with a long bow
> Than my predecessors. Carelessly I sing,
> But Phoebus lends me now and then a string. (VIII-CXXXVIII)

Under this purview 'your world' has to be reckoned 'topsy-turvy, twisted, crisp'd, and curl'd . . . turn'd inside, or drown'd' (IX-XXXVII). Juan, witness and participant, responds one way; Byron, or his interlocutor with perhaps Sterne in mind, another. The plenitude ('love, temper, travel, war') so mandates being told at velocity and in tactical switches from third to first person. The poem can acknowledge the risk of discursive 'rambling' as against any requirement simply to 'narrate' (IX-XLII). This irrepressibility as it shapes vision and versification affirms the continuing modern of *Don Juan*.

78   MODERNS – CHAUCER TO CONTEMPORARY FICTION

In her Preface to the 1831 re-issue of *Frankenstein* Mary Shelley famously explains the circumstances of composition: Lake Geneva bleak summer rain and cold, company with Percy Shelley and Byron and the challenge to compose a ghost story. The process for her was slow, the imagination seemingly resistant.

'Successive images' in due course take hold. 'Terror' beckons. 'Odious handywork' looms. The watchwords indicate the direction for which the novel has become universally known, namely Victor Frankenstein's act of creating his 're-animated' creature of human parts. This, Shelley's Preface further adds, for the scientist has been to transgress against 'the stupendous mechanism of the Creator of the world'. The creation of life through galvanism had led to the mirror birth of her own novel.[4]

The resulting narrative, Genesis turned into dark night, long has become staple gothic. The take-up proliferates from Robert Louis Stevenson's *The Strange Case of Dr. Jekyll and Mr. Hyde* (1886) to Daphne du Maurier's *Rebecca* (1938), or Poe's *The Narrative of Arthur Gordon Pym* (1838) to Toni Morrison's *Beloved* (1987). Screen incarnation puts the creature under hugely popular aegis. Universal Studio's black and white film (1931) projects in Boris Karloff's performance the archetypal image of sutured body, halting walk, block forehead. The figure has been regularly bracketed with screen Dracula, vampirism similarly transposed from Bram Stoker's *Dracula* (1897) and acted out by Bela Lugosi or Christopher Lee. In the cross-lights *Frankenstein*, the novel, often hovers beyond recognition.

One does not want exaggeration. Shelley's novel in no way matches the century's greater line of Jane Austen, George Eliot or the Brontës. The plot line has its creaks and improbabilities. The love affair between Victor Frankenstein and Elizabeth Lavenza leans towards sentimental piety. The detail of actual horror, for all the lamentations and shrieks, goes oddly missing. The prose reads dutifully. Reception, though not Shelley's doing, has blurred the very name Frankenstein, frequently attributing it to the creature as against the creator.

Allowing the extent to which the novel has been the subject of shock-horror myth, it continues to merit better engagement. Sheer novelty of imagination, science into science fiction, a hand at narrative patterning, diligent Alpine landscape, all weigh. Much, too, as *Frankenstein* deploys murder, lightning strike, the frisson of escape and pursuit across Europe and to the Arctic, it unfolds as speculative narrative. In an early letter from Captain Robert Walton to his sister Margaret he speaks of his 'voyage of discovery towards the northern pole' (13). The phrase, conveniently, opens into the novel's philosophic voyaging at large. When disclosing his story to Walton aboard the explorer-vessel as it quests for the Northwest Passage, Atlantic into Pacific, Victor reflects this greater will to discovery. 'To examine the causes of life, we must first have recourse to death', he alleges as if in remembrance of body parts taken from 'vaults and charnel-houses' (44). He expatiates on the prospect philosophically:

> Life and death appeared to me ideal bounds, should I first break through, and pour a torrent of light into our dark world. (47)

His human monster-creature, educated in chanced-upon book and treatise, becomes paradigmatic. He gains access to speech and formidable vocabulary. He acquires further learning from the blind cottager DeLacey and his family. He contemplates 'the strange system of human society' (124) with its 'property' (124) and 'differences of sexes' (125). The accumulated knowledge obliges him to reflect on his unique birthright:

> As I read, however, I applied much personally to my own feelings and condition. I found myself similar, yet at the same time strangely unlike to the beings concerning whom I read, and to whose conversation I was a listener . . . My person was hideous and my stature gigantic. What did this mean? Who was I? What was I? Whence did I come? What was my destination? Questions continually recurred, but I was unable to solve them. (134)

This rota, specific as it is to the plot line, confirms Shelley's desire to exceed mere shockwave. The creature cites Milton, and sees the reflection of himself in God's fallen angel envisioned in *Paradise Lost*. Shelley's daring scores. Her aim, discernibly, is modern revisitation of older equations. They embrace the search for absolutes (to which Walton is drawn also); the relationship of idealism to the actual; the unresolved enigmas of being.

In this ambition the novel merits coeval regard for design. *Frankenstein* draws upon, and figures, its alternations with notable assurance. The letters of Walton, his sister Margaret, Elizabeth as intended bride, the great friend Henri Clerval, the father Alphonse

Frankenstein, and Victor himself, give the novel competing sources of viewpoint. Confessions alternate to similar outcome. Justine Moritz falsely confesses to the murder of the child brother William, her self-martyring execution the outcome. The creature, hitherto having denied hearers for his confession, confesses the full story to Victor and to Walton before his last flight to 'the everlasting ices of the north' (222). Victor confesses to the paradox of being endlessly sealed in un-confession. The would-be benign tracker of life (the irony of his name not to be missed) is himself tracked by the eventual malevolent killer of the small girl, of Clerval, of William, and of Elizabeth. The launch, and abandonment in the lake, of a female body-partner for the creature, elicits the creature's synoptic verdict 'You are my creator, but I am your master' (179). Shelley makes something of a coup in rendering Victor and creature as doubles, *Doppelganger* alternates.

Notoriety has long assigned *Frankenstein* the reputation of classic horror. Melodrama, inevitably, contributes, but not at the expense of other narrative resource. 'The occurrences which are usually deemed marvellous' (19), as Walton describes them, justify being taken at wider parameter. The pathways to existential self-freedom and gender equality, echoed from Godwin and Wollstonecraft, Shelley embodies in the discourses of Victor and creature. Consciousness and its gyres recurs as query. Nature as against nurture win early surmise. The gains and pitfalls of science, whether genetics or technology, the novel puts under cautionary scrutiny. In these interplays, and their enduring figure of Frankenstein's creature, Mary Wollstonecraft Shelley's novel steps into the modern.

Thomas Love Peacock and the modern might at first sight seem the unlikely proposition. Do not his key satires attach only to Romanticism and the Regency? The shies may convey wit quick on its feet, wonderfully funny swerves, but do the novels amount to more? This hesitation recurs, though justly it has not prevailed.[5] For to consider *Nightmare Abbey,* or *Headlong Hall* (1815), *Crotchet Castle* (1831) and *Gryll Grange* (1861), mere *jeux d'esprit* falls appreciably short. On offer is Peacock's ear for how the one or another grandiose *idée fixe* trips up on idiosyncrasy. Comically, seriocomically, that holds foremost in *Nightmare Abbey*. Opinion long has favoured the conversation novel as descriptive genre. Conversation indeed abounds, an abundance of askew exchanges. They belong with the novel's companion dexterities. The abbey itself acts as first departure, home to 'dark lantern(s) of the spirit' in the epigraph from the Samuel Butler of *Hudibras*. Castellated, towered (one ivied and full of owls), its 'picturesque state of semi-delapidation' (39) makes for faultless pastiche. In making the abbey a time-past stronghold of the church militant, full of atmospheric shadow, Peacock immediately mimics Walpole's Otranto or Radcliffe's Udolpho. Hidden rooms, locked and false doors, cells, voices off, supposed ghosts, in all 'a spacious kennel' (40) in its owner's words, it makes the perfect architecture for the comic-ironic gothic of mind to follow.[6]

The cast list of credibly stylised types and humours, Peacock's antic Bunyan-ism, furnishes the parade. Mr Glowry Esq. and son Scythrop, names nothing if not playfully coagulated, engage from first mention. The elder, melancholic, attended by the lugubrious butler Raven, the valet Skellet and the grooms Mattocks and Graves, suffers 'phantoms of indigestion' (39) from a lost first love and comically embattled marriage. The younger, in Shelley's silhouette, also disappointed in love and weaned on the epistolary romanticism of *The Sorrows of Young Werther*, conceives a passion for reforming the world into 'a new model society' (47), 'a perfect republic' (47). That he becomes further jinxed by the two contrasting (and again pertinently named) women, Marionetta and Celena, distant re-incarnations of Shelley's Harriet Westbrook and Mary Wollstonecraft, adds farce to solemnity. Under the 'modern' hand Peacock brings to bear, the Glowrys and their fellow abbey-ists, variously transcendental, apocalyptic or panglossian, compete in intellectual foible with the exact degree of excess.

Nightmare Abbey, not to over-claim, remains skilled cartoon, Peacock's modern caricature. He very clearly knows the leading writer circle of the age, and its literature and thought, Coleridge, Byron, Shelley, likely Leigh Hunt, Kant from among the philosophers, and a bevy of cultists and evangelicals. His lance, acute but not savage (he is not Swift), takes aim most of all at affectation, forms of pretension. Mr Flosky, in this respect, assumes pride of place. His disposition Peacock locates with laconic relish. 'Mystery was his mental element' (44) holds his description. 'Transcendental darkness' (44) enwraps him. 'Light is a great enemy to mystery' (67) Peacock has him say as though mock-Coleridge, the illuminatus of *Biographia Literaria* who 'plunged into the central opacity of

Kantian metaphysics' (44). Flosky's taste for intellection supplies perfect grist for Peacock's parodic skills, 'modern' thought dealt with in less than deferential style.

The novel's other out-of-joint gentlemen (and lady) moderns fully point to larger catch. Mr Toobad, 'Manichaean Millenarian' (45), dispenses Calvinist woe as though confetti ('The Devil is come among us', 45, becomes his repeated tic). The Rev. Mr Larynx, opportunist, responds to the world with selfish adaptability ('Nothing came amiss to him', 45). The Hon. Mr Listless personifies Regency dandyism, Beau Brummell languor. Mr Hilary urges boundless good cheer as against Toobad's end-of-days fatalism. Mr Asteria, ichthyologist, and son Aquarius, in their quixotic search for mermaids and tritons, undermine the 'scientific' quest for the other-worldly exotic. Mr Cyprus, Byronesque, gives Peacock his chance to tease the alienated poet attracted to ever distant horizons (although he had once written un-admiringly of *Childe Harold*).

Nightmare Abbey remains inherently irregular, one-off. But the conversation format is not without literary cousinship, whether Herman Melville's Mississippi colloquium in *The Confidence Man* (1857) or Aldous Huxley's country-estate satire *Chrome Yellow* (1921). In *Crotchet Castle* Peacock writes in summary, 'A book that furnishes no quotations, is me judice, no book, – it is a plaything.' Without undue elevation of its accomplishment, *Nightmare Abbey*, and the perennial modern it embodies, goes a long way towards avoiding that risk.

Byron, Mary Shelley, Peacock. Their authorship evidently differs in direction and scale of achievement. But they each share one general overlap. *Don Juan* modernises the English literary epic, in scope, in voice. *Frankenstein* redraws the narrative map of gothic, less given to props of horror than the philosophic modern. *Nightmare Abbey* explores *comédie noire* as much of mind as plot. The yield of one era's modern for those to come is not to be missed.

Notes

1. Minor figure or otherwise, Peacock has been the subject of a monumental French study: Jean-Jacques Mayoux, *Un Epicurien anglais: Thomas Love Peacock*, Paris: Nizer et Bastard, 1933.

2. Byron scholarship has won strong scholarly attention. I have especially benefited from Leslie A. Marchand, *Byron's Poetry: A Critical Introduction*, Boston Houghton Mifflin Company, 1965; Harold Bloom, *The Visionary Company: A Reading of English Romantic Company*, Garden City, New York: Doubleday & Company, 1963; Andrew Rutherford, *Byron: A Critical Study*, Stanford, CA: Stanford University Press, 1961; and Graham Hough, *The Romantic Poets*, London: Hutchinson University Library, 1953.

3. This aspect of Byron is explored to great effect in Anne K. Mellor, *English Romantic Irony*, Cambridge, MA: Harvard University Press, 1980, 31–76.

4. These and all subsequent references are to *Frankenstein; or, the Modern Prometheus*, London: J. M. Dent, Everyman Edition, 1912, 2nd edn, 1922, vii–xii.

5. For a judicious reprimand to this characterisation of Peacock, see Howard Mills, *Peacock, His Circle and His Age*, Cambridge: Cambridge University Press, 1969.

6. All page references are to *Nightmare Abbey, Crotchet Castle*, ed. Raymond Wright, Harmondsworth, Middlesex: Penguin English Library, 1965.

CHAPTER 7

Like Nobody But Himself:
Modern Hazlitt

Robert Louis Stevenson was not alone in celebrating, and gener-ously envying, William Hazlitt's achievement when he wrote, 'Though we are mighty fine fellows nowadays, we cannot write like Hazlitt.'[1] The salute points to Hazlitt's case-for-case decisiveness of view caught in often magnetic prose. On the one hand the verve of expression extends to the Lake Poets and Shakespeare and paint-ers like Titian and Rembrandt, on the other to fisticuffs, sundials, Indian jugglers, Beau Brummell and dreams. 'Like nobody but him-self' belongs to his 'On the Character of Cobbett', as apt for himself as for the radical-minded author of the *Political Register* and *Rural Rides*.[2] The English essay has long had good fortune, Locke or Milton among forebears, Charles Lamb or Matthew Arnold from Hazlitt's century, Virginia Woolf or George Orwell subsequently. Hazlitt, the frequently embattled stance somehow intrinsic to the soar of his expressive strengths, belongs in the company. For across the array of literary and life interpretation he maintains a unique discursive modernity, truly nobody else's.

The title of Duncan Wu's biography, *William Hazlitt: The First Modern Man* (2008), could not be more apposite.[3] Wu, like Tom Paulin in *The Day-Star of Liberty: William Hazlitt's Radical Style* (1998), and others who have done much to uphold Hazlitt's reputa-tion, rightly draws attention to this quality of the modern.[4] To think Hazlitt other than modern in accent, a contemporaneous voice, does disservice. The range that includes *Characters of Shakespear's Plays* (1817), *Lectures on the English Poets* (1818), *Political Essays* (1819), *Table-Talk* (1821–2), *The Spirit of the Age* (1825) and *The Plain Speaker* (1826) hits home with exceptional force, fields of muscular opinion fully personal but never merely subjective.[5] His output, moreover, if not to advantage, extends into the strenuously

84

confessional *Liber Amoris* (1823) and four-part *Life of Napoleon Bonaparte* (1828–30). The essays will always prevail but, as these longer projects confirm, Hazlitt aspires to write the wider circle.

The track of Hazlitt's life requires little reminder. It begins with the Unitarian upbringing at Wem, Shropshire. The brief New England interlude follows, would-be Republicanism and Puritanism on his clergyman father's part. The influence of Locke, Rousseau and Burke begins early, with Hobbes to follow. Libertarianism and Jacobin celebration of the French Revolution and Bonaparte stay with him as convictions. Awe at the Coleridge he first meets in 1798, but eventual disaffection, recurs as lodestone. His lectures and considerable talent for painting, portrait and landscape, indicate alternative paths he might have followed with considerable chance of success. Hardscrabble setbacks recur. Frequent near-penury threatens even as he takes to his pen. Against the odds he manages to fashion some of the most stirring literary critique and pockets of observation in the English language. He seeks income as jobbing reviewer and journalist. Quarrels, scandal, become a busy and much-pressed stream.

The marriages end in divorce, to Sarah Stoddard with whom he found a period of tranquillity in their home at Winterslow on the Salisbury Plain, and briefly, to the widowed Isabella Bridgwater, an alliance more of convenience than love. Midlife sexual infatuation with Sarah Walker, young daughter of his landlord in Southampton Row, London, and the ensuing brouhaha which follows publication of *Liber Amoris*, brings on breakdown. His alertness to the political as well as the literary currents of his times is registered in *Political Essays* and *The Spirit of the Age*. Bentham and Godwin typically serve for subjects of interest, Castlereagh and Malthus for targets. Of his writer friends the Lambs, Charles and Mary, and Keats hold his affection. The wear and illnesses that led to death in his sparse Soho lodging in 1850 add up to a career prone to volatility, acclaim and margin.

Correspondence, both public and private, shows his fractious genius, the obdurate stance often to the point of distemper. The essays have a share of this but not to the point of inhabiting mastery. In fact, they give impetus. The modern lodged within Hazlitt, and which presses into his very style, draws from his rare degree of attentive viewpoint, be it literature and visual art, power and the state, character and fashion. He would inveigh against abstraction, authorship or canvas that as he saw it did not originate in lived actuality. A quartet of his essays offer guiding points, notably for how they alight on the dynamics of writing itself.

Hazlitt rarely better sets out his author's stall than in 'On Familiar Style' (1821), a mantra of sorts, his formulation as to writing 'a genuine familiar or truly English style'.[6] His essay enacts the self-same prerequisites he lays down as essential: 'vigour' as against 'verbiage', the 'familiar and natural' as against the 'mechanical, conventional, vapid, pedantic in style and execution' (212–13):

> As an author, I endeavour to employ plain words and popular modes of construction, as were I a chapman and dealer, I should common weights and measures. (208)

To an extent a certain disingenuousness applies. Hazlitt executes his 'plain words', his 'popular modes', with formidable originality. He chastises the examples of Dr Johnson for sameness of style and holds up Shakespeare's Ancient Pistol as a warning against 'profusion of barbarous epithets' (212). He reserves praise for Elia, Charles Lamb, as 'the only imitator of English style I can read with pleasure' (210). The modern is to be found in the eloquence of circumstantial voice, not in the 'tall phantoms of words' or 'circuitous metaphors' (213).

'My First Acquaintance with the Poets' (1823), essentially Hazlitt's encounter with Coleridge, abounds in vernacular detail. Wintry branches, Welsh mountain blue tops, sunrays and puddles, frame his exhilaration at the poet's gift of talk as it frees Hazlitt from 'my understanding' that hitherto has lain 'dumb and brutish' (43–4). Coleridge, indicatively, is owed the release of 'language to express myself' (44). His preaching, after Hazlitt's next ten-mile walk through mud and under 'cold, raw, comfortless' weather to hear him, swoops down upon his follower as though from 'an eagle dallying in the wind' (45). Coleridge is to be likened to a Murillo or Velázquez figure while at the same time he is to be recalled feeding on Welsh mutton and turnips. In similar vein, and as the account moves from Shropshire to Nether Stowey, Hazlitt grounds remembrance of Coleridge on Hume, or on Godwin, or on *The Lyrical Ballads*, in lane-walking, cottage-smoke and more mud. The portrait thereby steers high and low, Coleridge the poet-philosopher whose discourse

WILLIAM HAZLITT   87

holds domain and the Coleridge of '*matter-of-factness*' who 'makes
havoc of a Cheshire cheese' (58–9). Hazlitt works these stops ease-
fully, the calibration exact. He writes historical remembrance but
only as though modern to the touch.

It perhaps sounds perverse to turn for literary touchstone to
'On The Pleasure of Painting' (1820, reprinted 1821). Even more
perverse has to be Hazlitt's declaration of preference for canvas or
art-paper over script and that he brings to bear his seasoned cur-
riculum as writer. Thinking back on his literary and other essays he
declares a paradoxical un-relish:

> I have not much pleasure in writing these Essays, or in reading
> them afterwards: though I now and then meet with a phrase
> that I like, or a thought that strikes me as a true one . . . After
> I have once written on a subject, it goes out of my mind: my
> feelings about it have been melted down into words, and *them*
> I forget. (67–8)

The slaps at the sedentary act of writing, chair to table, verb to
paragraph, embody symptomatic contrariety, the writer writing to
de-estimate his chosen path. Contrast lies in painting, choice of colour and pigment, use of eye, understanding of light. Hazlitt has
his predilections, Correggio or da Vinci over Rubens or Van Dyck.
Each painter, nonetheless, commands the 'delightful never-ending
progress to perfection' (75). The physicality of easel and palette,
having acted as vehicles to 'new truth', 'new observation' (74), help
further in the avoidance of 'abstract ideas' (76). Hazlitt may well
think painting the greater pull, but with model fluency it has taken
the essayist to capture precisely the competing allure of brushstroke.

The paradox of 'A Farewell to Essay-Writing' (1828) resides in
the fact that it again stands as itself the wholly engaging familiar
essay. 'Food, warmth, sleep, and a book; these are all I at present
ask' (482) reads the opening prescription, true maybe yet given
Hazlitt's life as author short of the whole truth. The essay, against
itself, professes to privilege life, and live Nature, above the written
page. Whether in refutation of Leigh Hunt's recent unflattering portrait ('I am neither a buffoon, a fop, nor a Frenchman, which Mr
Hunt would have me be', 486), or simply fatigued by his unremit-
ting pen, he implies that he is contentedly out to pasture.[7] His times,
thus, resort to Nature as miraculous theatre, the comfort of the

natural away from it all. He invokes 'clouds sailing from the west', 'a neighbouring wood', 'slender branches of birch trees', 'a whirring pheasant' and even 'a dead woodpigeon' (483). These 'lovely living hues' exceed museum Titians. They suggest 'Claude Lorraine skies', serve as 'my true classics', and eclipse 'my speculations' (490–1). Valedictory in purpose, the essay brims with writer confidence of image, in sum and contrarily, Hazlitt the pre-eminent modern essayist composing his unlikely farewell to the essay.

As engaged literary critic Hazlitt continues to win repute, never without point of view, alert, disputatious. Choice is plentiful. 'The Lake School' (1818), typically, opens with a punch. The acclaimed 'lakers' are not to be held 'sacred from criticism' or exempt from 'faults' (215). The essay 'Mr. Wordsworth' (1818), accordingly, allows for 'the man of genius' but gripes at Wordsworth's giving way to his 'homely Muse' (219), which 'strives to reduce all things to a standard' (220). Nature becomes a kind of enclosed parish register of mountain, daisy, cuckoo, linnet's nest, torn outdoor cloak and rock lichen, in which every small item is 'significant' (222–3). Grandeur of scene, moral awakening, pertain, but as though through the single filter. Wordsworth's 'solitary' musing, his 'daily converse with the face of nature' (222), in Hazlitt's view, exacts its price ('his poetry has no other source or character', 222). The poet absents itself from the cross-plies and ambiguities of larger human concourse, even despite 'delightful passages' as in *The Excursion* (225). *Lyrical Ballads*, whatever its impact, is weakened by an 'unaccountable mixture of seeming simplicity and real abstruseness'(220). Idolatry has further inhibited critique, especially of Wordsworth's establishmentarian tilt. Whether or not Hazlitt sees Wordsworth, or the *Ballads*, aright, his criticism confirms active brim of mind. The modern in Hazlitt calls out for livelier, un-cowed evaluation, the hail to Wordsworth having become complacent, altogether too routine.

'Mr. Coleridge' possesses the same double-edge. The essay shows enormous funds of respect ('On whatever question or author you speak, he is prepared to take up the theme with advantage', 233). Yet reservation accompanies ('he is trying to subject the Muse to *transcendental* theories: in his abstract reasoning he misses his way by strewing it with flowers', 234). He lauds Coleridge the talker, his devastating command of philosophical cogitation. But he finds 'The Ancient Mariner' the only poem 'he could with confidence put

WILLIAM HAZLITT 89

into any person's hands, on whom we wished to impress a favourable idea of his extraordinary powers' (240). More egregious still has to be Coleridge's prose ('If our author's poetry is inferior to his conversation, his prose is utterly abortive' 241). Hazlitt's posture has about it genuine boldness, willingness to defend his stand. He finally comes to think Coleridge marred by abstract dryness, genealogies of thought over imagination. These, for him, might be designated the un-modern Coleridge ('It was a misfortune to any man of talent to be born in the latter end of the last century', 243).

Hazlitt's lowered eye, and cogency, runs through virtually all his critical offerings. Southey as poet-intellectual in his retreat from approval of Wat Tyler radicalism to self-advancement under royalty incurs his reprimand as 'a prude and a scold' (245). The poet George Crabbe, he judges, comes over wearingly ('There is here no flights of fancy, no illusions of sentiment, no tinsel of words', 247). Dr Johnson, for whom 'We have a high respect', attracts notable chastisement, and in conjunction with Shakespeare. 'All his ideas were cast in a given mould' attests Hazlitt of Johnson's *Preface to the Plays of William Shakespeare*, not helped by 'cumbrous phraseology'. Hazlitt's succinctness, whether or not be intended contrast, strikes home – 'Johnson's understanding dealt only in round numbers: the fractions were lost upon him' (267).

Shakespeare himself, the supreme modern, unsurprisingly draws some of the best of Hazlitt's modern hand. Typical is the following passage from 'On Shakespear and Milton' in *Lectures on the English Poets* (1818):

> The striking peculiarity of Shakespear's mind was its generic quality, its power of communication with all other minds – so that it contained a universe of thought and feeling within itself, and had no one peculiar bias, or exclusive excellence more than another.[8]

Shakespeare so embodies the permanent modern – open, encompassing, the abiding aspiration for Hazlitt himself. The thirty-plus essays of *Characters of Shakespear's Plays* propose a Shakespeare of the unchanging now, ever alive in the present. Hazlitt nonetheless can express misgivings about the poems and sonnets ('The author seems all the time to be thinking of his verses, and not of his subject') or make the surprising comparison ('we do not like Shakespear's poems, because we like his plays').[9] These commentaries stir with acuity, arrest, not least when contestatory. Among the tragedies, *Lear* has him recognise the king's fatal presumption while in shared extent the sympathy he arouses:

> It is his rash haste, his violent impetuosity, his blindness to every thing but the dictates of his passions or affections, that produces all his misfortunes, that aggravates his impatience of them, that enforces our pity for him. (119)

Hamlet likewise elicits comment striking in its modern temper, the prince less the appointed revenger than vehicle of inner human thought:

> Hamlet is a name; his speeches and sayings but the idle coinage of the poet's brain. What, then, are they not real? They are as real as our own thoughts. Their reality is in the reader's mind. It is *we* who are Hamlet. (79)

Macbeth moves towards a sense of irreality, at once 'tragical' yet 'preternatural' (12), its format 'a huddling together of fierce extremes' (18). *Othello* as play contemplates 'the alternate ascendancy of different passions', pathologies of both 'fondest love' and 'the madness of hatred' (34).

The histories have him describing the Falstaff of *Henry IV* as 'carrying his own larder about with him' (146), his wit 'for the most part a masterly presence of mind' (147); the Henry of *Henry V* as a 'very amiable monster' (158); and the Gloucester of *Richard III* as 'not a man striving to be great, but to be greater than he is' (174). The comedies and romances inspire ongoing keenness of response, whether censure or praise. *Love's Labour's Lost* does not make the grade ('If we were to part with any of the author's comedies, it should be this', 225). *As You Like It* deserves applause for its cast and setting ('the very air of the place seems to breathe a spirit of philosophical poetry', 234). Of the late plays *The Tempest* ranks as 'one of the most original and perfect of Shakespear's productions' (88), from Prospero, the 'stately magician', to Caliban, 'the essence of grossness without a particle of vulgarity' (90). Across these, and the spectrum of Shakespeare's drama, Hazlitt confirms his operational, and inarguably modern, intelligence.

Hazlitt and the world, as it were, amply exhibits this same forte in a number of classic essays. 'The Fight' (1822), his portrait of the journey from Chancery Lane to Hungerford Common to watch the illegal prizefight between the butcher Bill Neate and Tom Hickman, known as the Gaslight Man, exceeds anything in New Journalism 'modern' sports-writing:

> Reader, have you ever seen a fight? If not you have a pleasure to come, at least if it is a fight like that between the Gas-man and Bill Neate.[10]

Wonderfully vivid, re-enactive of coach discomfort, inns, company and talk, and then the outlaw combat in full kinetic colour, it imports the breathing present into the essay. The there-and-back, from the rumour in the *Hole in the Wall* eatery and his link-up with Joe Toms, gives the air of anticipation. The near misses of finding different carriages to get him to the venue relay rising tension. The 'knock-down blows' of the fight (92), the flurry of blows and feints, complete the brilliant reportorial spectacle.

Hazlitt assembles his material as to participant-writer born. He cites his own training ('exercise and abstinence') and morning diet ('A yoke of an egg with a spoonful of rum') in contrast with his pestering 'indigestion' (83–4). He puts himself amid the club and coffee house 'social chat', the betting odds ('About two thousand pounds were pending', 87), and the crowd from upper-class swells to artisans. Round for round commentary accompanies, the gladiators local but likened to Achilles and Hector. Body weight, punch, stagger, feint, bravery, blood, 'red ruin' face, a right eye 'closed in dingy blackness', and the fall of Neate ('He was not like an actual man, but like a preternatural, spectral appearance', 93), all in turn fuse. Fight over, there remains the reference to other pugilists within memory, among them James Belcher, Gentleman Jackson and Bill Richmond, who he names as 'my old master' (88). Massive 'high spirits' prevail throughout his return to London (97). For Hazlitt, the occasion and its actors amounts to vernacular *Aeneid*, Homer updated, modern to a fault.

Action-writing, if that fits, has another rousing incarnation in 'The Indian Jugglers' (1821). Hazlitt again assumes participatory mode, equally the diarist of himself and his reactions as of the jugglers. He holds, too, to his repeated point of the higher standing of animation in life over script; yet his view is conveyed triumphantly

92   MODERNS – CHAUCER TO CONTEMPORARY FICTION

within the drama of that script. The essay celebrates athletic perfection, brass-balls-in-the-air juggled with the grace he praises as 'beauty triumphing over skill' (119). He moves out to examples of other grace, feats more than mere cleverness or sleight-of-hand, be it great portrait painting, the renowned surgery of John Hunter, or best public eloquence. Especial acclaim is reserved for the game of fives, which he himself played and relished, and whose skilled players he celebrates in names like his contemporaries John Cavanagh and John Davies.

In characteristically articulate style he imagines he sees the mirror of his supposed imperfections:

> It makes me ashamed of myself. I ask what there is that I can do as well as this. Nothing . . . I can write a book: so can many others who have never learned to spell. What abortions are these Essays! The utmost I can do is to write a description of what this fellow can do. What errors, what ill-pieced transitions, what crooked reasons, what lame conclusions! How little is made out, and that little how ill! (119–20)

The 'utmost I can do' that obtains, and it is hard to think Hazlitt is being disingenuous, does infinitely more than well enough. Abortive would be the last word to describe the essays. His transitions of sight and sentence come about with fluidity. Conclusions are anything but lame, convenient signings-off. Mere reportage, as usual, does not cover the workings of the piece. The modern jugglery lies in the measure of Hazlitt's writing, his own literary juggling in kind with that of 'white dress and turbaned' performers before his rapt gaze (118) and of the art of the different exemplary creative figures he names in association with them.

'On a Sun-Dial' (1827) displays the similar conjunction of perspectives, in this case Time and its ambit considered through the sighting of a specific Brenta River Venetian dial. Taking stock of the dial from aboard his boat it dispenses for Hazlitt bucolic serenity. 'Cares of life' recede. 'Infinity and eternity' promise. 'Duration' hangs in the air and shadow, the implication being 'we should scarce be conscious of our existence' (169). A litany of other timepieces pale by comparison, the ornamental French clocks he abhors, tiresome pocket watches, irritating chimers of the hour, even Mr Shandy's ill-timed clock in the begetting of Tristram. The exception is to be heard in the village bells of Italy or Salisbury Plain as against those of cathedrals like Rouen and Cologne ('hoarse with counting the flight of ages', 175–6) and of dogged Holland ('Time in Holland is a foolish old fellow', 176). The time sounds he relishes hark back to older settled life, those of the English rural church and which he cites Coleridge of having thought them 'the poor man's music' (175). He acknowledges the river experience as reverie, cause to be 'proud of killing time with thought, nay even without thinking' (178). Hazlitt, modern as ever, in effect has the essay reflect himself as time's figure as much as that of the sight in the Venice river, the one dial for the other.

'Montaigne' (1819), short tribute to his admired doyen of essayists, bears another implicit mirror of Hazlitt himself. The opening sentence easily applies:

> The great merit of Montaigne was, that he may be said to have been the first who had the courage as an author to say what he felt as a man. (270)

The temptation arises to think how Montaigne would have written a reverse panegyric. Hazlitt, too, assumes his place as a 'man of original mind' (270) who has 'sowed the seed and cleared away the rubbish ... even where others have cultivated and decorated the soil to a greater degree of nicety and perfection' (271). The fuller estimate comes yet closer:

> He did not, in the abstract character of an author, undertake to say all that could be said upon a subject, but what in his capacity as an inquirer after truth he happened to know about it. He was neither a pedant nor bigot. He neither supposed that he was bound to know all things, nor that all things were bound to conform to what he had fancied or would have them to be. (270)

The comparison might slightly flatter Hazlitt, but the mutual attributes extend: 'inexpressible frankness', 'power', and most of relevance, 'this new way of writing' (271). Montaigne has his fellow-spirit in Hazlitt, their authorship pledged to capturing the world in terms recognisably not simply new but modern.

Notes

1. Robert Louis Stevenson, *Virginibus Puerisque and Other Papers*, 1881. Stevenson himself acknowledged taking Hazlitt for one of his exemplars for style and range of topic.
2. 'On the Character of Cobbett', *Table Talk, Essays on Men and Manners*, 1822.
3. Duncan Wu, *William Hazlitt: the First Modern Man*, Oxford: Oxford University Press, 2008.
4. Tom Paulin, *The Day-Star of Liberty: William Hazlitt's Radical Style*, London: Faber & Faber, 1998. It would be remiss not to mention A. C. Grayling, *The Quarrel of the Age: The Life and Times of William Hazlitt*, London: Weidenfeld & Nicholson, 2000.
5. I have retained throughout Hazlitt's spelling of Shakespeare as Shakespear.
6. 'On Familiar Style', *William Hazlitt: Selected Writings*, ed. Ronald Blythe, Harmondsworth, Middlesex: Penguin Books, 1970, 206. All references are to this edition unless otherwise specified.
7. Hunt, however, was in general a fierce advocate for Hazlitt. His swipe came about as the result of a temporary spat to do with Hazlitt's criticism of Wordsworth and Coleridge.
8. 'On Shakespear and Milton', *Lectures on the English Poets*, reprinted *William Hazlitt: Selected Writings*, 273.
9. Page references are to *Characters of Shakespear's Plays*, London: J. M. Dent & Sons, Everyman Edition, 1906, 264.
10. Page references return to *William Hazlitt: Selected Writings*, 87. One unexpected tribute is to be found in Norman Mailer, *King of the Hill: The Fight of the Century*, New York: New American Library, 1971. Mailer would acknowledge the footfall of Hazlitt in his account of the Ali–Frazier contest.

CHAPTER 8

Out of Victorianism: Samuel Butler, Lytton Strachey, Ford Madox Ford

Victorianism can serve only for an approximate category, the abbreviation of over sixty years of highly various history and culture. The single designation has long done wide duty: industry, empire, reform, family, class, patriarchy, a literary constellation that embraces Dickens, George Eliot and Matthew Arnold.[1] By the next century it had become an Age, apportioned into High and Low, and to be still admired but increasingly opened to critique. Few voices more intimately reflect the latter contour than Samuel Butler, author of a landmark fictional biography, or Lytton Strachey, Bloomsbury master of ceremonies, or Ford Madox Ford, contrarian novelist in his organisation of narrative as of sexual theme. Their break-through, or rather break-out, resides in indicative 'modern' texts, *The Way of All Flesh* (1873–5, published 1903), *Eminent Victorians* (1918) and *The Good Soldier* (1915).[2]

Butler's interests, diverse to a fault, are to be found in the 'undiscovered countries' of his utopian *Erewhon* (1872) and its sequels, the dozen other full-length works with their interests in theology, evolution, Homer and Shakespeare, and in his untiring Notebooks. Symptomatically he writes in his *Notebooks*:

> Everyman's mind is an unknown land to himself, so that we need not be at such pains to frame a mechanism of adventure for getting to undiscovered countries. We have not far to go before we reach them. They are, like the Kingdom of Heaven, within us.[3]

In Strachey, Victorianism falls under finely sceptical gaze, whether upon 'eminent' heroes less statuesque than conventionally thought

96 MODERNS – CHAUCER TO CONTEMPORARY FICTION

or, almost affectionately, upon Victoria herself. His account in *Queen Victoria* (1921) carries his characteristic tone:

> In the dazzled imagination of her subjects Victoria soared aloft towards the regions of divinity through a nimbus of purest glory. Criticism fell dumb; deficiencies which, twenty years earlier, would have been universally admitted, were now as universally ignored. That the nation's idol was a very incomplete representative of the nation was a circumstance that was hardly noticed, and yet it was conspicuously true.[4]

Ford Madox Ford, against Victorian sexual discretion, writes a novel bold in the anatomy of desire, and fittingly for a literary apostle of the modern, duplicitous in narrator and telling. His view of the age into which he was born suggests farewell to preceding habits and a hail to hitherto untrodden territory:

> They were simple, earnest people, those early Victorians, and had not yet learnt the trick of avoiding disturbing thoughts and sights.[5]

Each of these writers has attracted recognition of this bid for a changed dispensation. In the case of Butler we have V. S. Pritchett's opinion:

> *The Way of All Flesh* is one of the time bombs of literature. One thinks of it lying in Butler's desk at Clifford's Inn for thirty years, waiting to blow up the Victorian family and with it the whole great pillared and balustraded edifice of the Victorian novel.[6]

For Strachey, his pre-eminent scholar Michael Holroyd gives full regard to the radicalism of the best-known work:

> *Eminent Victorians* had, of course, been his fiercest and most influential piece of polemics, dissipating the atrocious fog of Victorian sentiment and exposing much of its sham folklore.[7]

For Ford's novel, criticism alights on darker truths beneath the rules:

> The Victorians averted their gaze from the ugliness and injustices before them. Concealments were fostered by the social grace,

the amenities and urbanities, the decorum so highly prized . . . It is this legacy of his own generation that Ford examines in *The Good Soldier*.[8]

Heirs to the private as to the public face of Victorianism, Butler, Strachey and Ford give their shrift to the age and its assumptions, each a fellow adept in its 'modern' demolition.

Early into *The Way of All Flesh* Butler virtually lets the mask drop. He has the novel's ostensible narrator, Edward Overton, observe:

> Every man's work, whether it be literature or music or pictures or architecture or anything else, is always a portrait of himself, and the more he tries to conceal himself the more clearly will his character appear in spite of him. I may very likely be condemning myself, all the time that I am writing this book, for I know that whether I like it or no I am portraying myself more surely than I am portraying any of the characters I set before the reader. (91–2)

Butler writing Overton writing Ernest Pontifex so enlarges the notion of the biographical novel, the life of Ernest under the one guise and itself under the guise of another. If Overton and Ernest share narrative space, narrator and narrated, they triangulate surreptitiously with Butler himself. Whose 'biography', or for that matter, whose 'autobiography', is it really? The sources in Butler's personal history have been amply documented, but there remains opportunity to emphasise the 'modern' tactics behind his routeways into human behaviour.

The novel's timeline is clear enough, from 1835 for the birth of Ernest through to the biography's close in 1867. Butler, however, is not about chronology. His subject is psychodrama, the evolving inner pathology of self. Ernest's Pontifex lineage acts as 'historical' preface. There follow, in increasing density, his vexed boyhood under the blinkered Rev. Theobald Pontifex and acquiescent mother Christina, grim public school, Cambridge, ordination, prison sentence, marriage and fatherhood, and final escape into bachelorhood and travel. Ernest emerges at once the insider and outrider ('I am an Ishmael by instinct as much as by accident and circumstances', 408), be it at the one remove his own story's custodian.

98   MODERNS – CHAUCER TO CONTEMPORARY FICTION

That holds despite Overton's role, starting from genealogist ('This brings us to the second generation of the Pontifex family with whom we need to concern ourselves', 37) and timekeeper ('And now I will continue my story', 115). His incursions tease the issue of who has rights of author ('I am told, by the way, that I must have let my memory play me one of the tricks it does play me', 147). Epigrams likewise fall under shared domain ('Some people say that their school days were the happiest of their lives. They may be right but I always look with suspicion upon those I hear saying this', 221). When Overton acknowledges having re-imagined scenes, interpolated correspondence, and even reproduced Ernest's essay on Greek drama, whose authorship lies to hand? It is Overton, himself the writer, who archly observes of Ernest the emergent writer: 'I want him to write like other people, and not offend so many of his readers; he says . . . that he must write as he does or not at all' (428–9). Butler, if not to all tastes, again lies not so hidden.

The modern in Butler has manifestation in the energy of opinion, the look of involvement and disaccord in a host of current quarrels. None in *The Way of All Flesh* takes greater priority than piety about hearth and family ('Certainly there is not inherent love for the family system on the part of nature herself', 131). Overton vents his disdain for Pontifex-Victorian parenting ('the long and savage cruelty with which [Ernest] had been treated in childhood', 297). Theobald Pontifex's thrashings of his son and Dr Skinner's prescription of narrow scriptural doctrine at Roughborough School bespeak a view of the world damaging in its treatment of the young human spirit. In the support of Althea Pontifex, the kindly aunt, a freethinker, Ernest has the glimpse of a better pathway into adulthood, but she (too conveniently?) dies early. The literal imprisonment he undergoes in consequence of the curate Pryer's financial connivance has its analogy in the enclosures of his life before eventual freedom.

Butler's surrogation to Overton, and he to Ernest, gives him a large platform, not the least that 'no system based on absolute certainty was possible' (351). Religion of the stripe Ernest encounters comes in for especial rebuke. Anglicanism's Broad and High Church divide, the popular evangelism of the fervid Mr Hawke in Cambridge, or the taste for confession and celibacy over vernacular mission work of the duplicitous Mr Pryer in London, leads only to dismay. Disenchantment grows with the Christianity preached in London's parishes in proportion to awareness of how little, Ernest comes to recognise, he understands the lower-class life being evangelised. 'Marriage and the family system' (409) likewise stir misgiving. Butler/Overton portrays it in Ernest's case as domestic imprisonment, as he transitions from contented small-shop business life with the village girl Ellen, his bibulous wife, and into release via the (let it be said contrived) chance of an invalid wedding contract.

Other motifs gather, some at the edge of eccentricity. Butler has Ernest address evolution and the role of fossils and geology and the implication for the timescale alleged in the Bible. He assigns recognition to Lamarck as evolutionist as much as Darwin. Heredity he interprets as a form of cellular memory to influence not just the physical body but human character as born out through the Pontifex generations. Subsequent directions of Freudian analysis of childhood and related trauma, have their antecedents. Lesser, if still obsessive, focus dwells on the role of money in life, the spectacle of religious conversion, the likely prohibition of tobacco under Pauline edict, and Handel's baroque the better over Bach and, later, Beethoven. For some these add up to miscellany, for others the turn of lively appetite.

The Way of All Flesh rarely wins all stakes. E. M. Forster saw it possessed of virtues but veering close to uncertain venture under 'the god called Muddle'.[9] Many of the issues the novel engages with continue in debate if, allegedly, under skewed eye. Their modernity makes for one kind of claim. Butler's originality of format makes for another. It is this dual Butler who holds ground, his will towards the modern in both ideas and text. William Maxwell provides relevant summary:

> Every contemporary novelist with a developed sense of irony is probably in some measure, directly or indirectly, indebted to Butler ... who had the misfortune to be a twentieth-century man born in the year 1835.[10]

Lytton Strachey's Preface to *Eminent Victorians* leaves little to doubt. Prior 'Standard Biographies' require jettisoning. The need has arrived for 'brevity', 'freedom of spirit', 'impartiality', accounts free of all 'tedious panegyric' and 'funereal barbarism':

> I have attempted through the medium of biography, to present some Victorian visions to the modern eye ... In the lives of an ecclesiastic, an educational authority, a woman of action, and

100 MODERNS – CHAUCER TO CONTEMPORARY FICTION

a man of adventure, I have sought to examine and elucidate certain fragments of the truth which took my fancy and lay to my hand.[11]

'To the modern eye' governs as key.

The eminences under review, Cardinal Manning, Florence Nightingale, Dr Thomas Arnold and General Gordon, Strachey fully recognises for their redoubtable presence. Indeed he counts on it. Of necessity, and as customary with Strachey, the satiric instinct takes over. 'Contradictious' is Strachey's word for Gordon. It applies equally well to all chosen four. They have towered for the age while, he makes clear, exhibiting quirk, not fissure exactly but want of congruity. The wit treads nimbly but unmistakably, Victorianism never without inexhaustible vigour but in its notables slightly cracked. No longer is Victorianism to be used as yardstick to bemoan subsequent fallings-away. The modern, recognisably, has become standpoint, necessary rebuke to assumed convention.

Throughout, Strachey keeps up deft ironic pressure. Writing of Anglicanism under threat of change from the Oxford and Tractarian movements, his observation is sly ('For many generations the Church of England has slept the sleep of the ... comfortable', 19). Manning's comportment he portrays as that of politician as much as prelate. 'Omnipotent Righteousness', duly capitalised, is his phrase for the godhead favoured by Florence Nightingale. Dr Arnold, ruminating on a youth who shot and killed an officer during the Paris Revolution of 1830, has Strachey impute to him the thought 'such were the alarming results of insufficient whipping' (170). Remembering Gordon amid the later phases of the Sudanese episode he alights on the General's 'strange exhilarations' (229). These commentaries-in-small exhibit Strachey the inerasable wielder of knife. The chosen quartet, to whom he brings meticulous swathes of detail, yields him every return.

Manning, on becoming Cardinal, receives the accolade from his Vatican supporter Monsignor Talbot, 'I believe your appointment was specially directed by the Holy Ghost', about which Strachey archly comments, 'Manning himself was apparently of the same opinion' (74). Opening the portrait under the rubric of 'its interest for the modern reader', Strachey suggests the dual focus, namely 'the light which [Manning's] career throws upon the spirit of the age, and the psychological problems suggested by his inner history' (13). The

SAMUEL BUTLER, LYTTON STRACHEY, FORD MADOX FORD 101

widower Anglican, whose conversion and eventual Cardinalship has him negotiating English and Vatican politics, stirs the comment, 'Power had come to him at last; and he seized it with all the avidity of a born autocrat' (76). Newman is invoked as ecclesiastical mirror, although the saintly but 'half-effeminate' Old School Catholic. Manning, as visible in fashionable dining room as in selective parish round, for Strachey works diligently within his limits, to be spoken of as he notes a half-plausible successor to Pius IX. The valedictory of 'The Cardinal's memory is a dim thing today' (108), mock-rueful, cuts matters down to size.

Florence Nightingale, whose nursing and hospital reform Strachey thinks 'heroic', 'extraordinary', that of 'an eagle' (126), he sees as having been 'getting ready' from birth (116). He approves her often repeated wish to relinquish The Lady with the Lamp image, but cannot resist, whisperingly, to have her perceived as 'the lady Superintendent . . . at her task' (122). He lists the busy parade of her birth to wealth, fierce Christian vocation, and work in bringing medical care to the soldiery at the Crimea's Scutari hospital in the wake of the Battle of Balaclava, and then far beyond. Likewise he gives acknowledgement to her public renown, Gladstone's visits to her and her visits to the Queen, a thousand committees, correspondence and articles. He so writes judiciously that 'she combined the intense vitality of a domineering woman of the world with the mysteries and romantic quality of myth' (152). But the edge persists. He enumerates 'the acrimony of her nature' (158), the obdurate spinsterhood, the ruling dispensations from her sofa in South Street, London. He performs at his most symptomatic in his view of her faith: 'She felt towards Him as she might have felt towards a glorified sanitary engineer' (154).

'He became a celebrity; he became at last a great man' (184). The impact of Thomas Arnold, D.D. would not be said to have been lost on Strachey any more than on Arnold's own Victorian peers. The portrait Strachey develops works at a slant, whether Arnold the muscular Christian ('All who knew him . . . were impressed by the earnestness of his religious convictions', 165), the reforming public school headmaster of Rugby ('He would treat the boys at Rugby as Jehovah had treated the Chosen People', 168), or the voluminous Professor of Modern History at Oxford in 1841 with an aversion to the insufficiently 'moralist' Edward Gibbon. Strachey treats Arnold's various convictions with his usual scepticism. 'The

Christian Gentleman' is to be the aim of good schooling. Greek and Latin but not science or French should dominate the syllabus. His Sunday sermons expound the 'general principles both of his own conduct and that of the Almighty' (173) with their aim, eyebrow-raisingly, to show 'the bearing of the incidents of Jewish history in the sixth century B.C. upon the conduct of English schoolboys in 1830' (173). Arnold's 'sense of moral evil' (226) invites note aided by his contribution as 'the founder of athletics and the worship of good form' (187). In the teasing final paragraph Strachey himself might be recognised as one of the schoolboys 'who wears the wrong clothes and takes no interest in football' (188) – football, here, in fact rugby. The insinuation of himself as being one of Arnold's successful 'modern' failures is not to be missed.

General Gordon, 'solitary English gentleman'(189) with the 'look of almost childish sincerity'(189), comes in for similar demur. Strachey has claim to have been among the first to doubt Gordon of Khartoum as historical monument. He reiterates the set-piece heroisation, Gordon the military genius, the Christian paragon, the colonial martyr. He attends to the career in full register: army officer in the Crimean War, service in China in the wake of the Taiping Rebellion, charity and fort-construction work in Gravesend, employment in Equatoria under the Egyptian pashas, and antislavery activism. The eventual Governorship in the Sudan, and death at the hands of the Mahdi's soldiers after any amount of mix-up in policy by the English Foreign and War offices, becomes the climax. Into these strands Strachey weaves his view of Gordon's 'eccentricities' (203). He implies the death wish in Gordon. He hints at the vexed and wholly un-discharged bachelor sexuality and love of 'boys' (198). There is the military man's hatred of domesticity and longing for 'danger' (199). Bouts of submissive spirituality co-exist with likely private drinking. The summary he offers assembles these competing directions: 'In the depths of Gordon's soul there were intertwining contractions – intricate recesses where egoism and renunciation melted into one another' (200). Strachey has him the 'supreme lord of the Sudan' yet also the unclothed emperor and even a little 'off his head' (266).

Strachey's chosen subjects hitherto leave little margin for preservation of the status quo. On his part disaffection begins from the very title of his book, eminence a term of unwarranted inflation. In varying measure, and despite the general esteem, they have lived lives somehow out of focus, at irregular angle. Judicious estimation or unfair pique, this puts the stalwarts of a presiding recent age under suspicion, the sharp flint of Strachey's modern disclosure.

Ford Madox Ford as modern, as modernist, draws from a renowned compendium of identities. His Anglo-German family meant early cosmopolitanism, fluency in languages. Ford Madox Brown, his Pre-Raphaelite grandfather, gave him exposure to the painter's studio and the visual arts. The energies behind over thirty novels are proverbial, to include the Tietjens tetrology, especially *No More Parades* (1925), and collaboration with Joseph Conrad on *The Inheritors* (1901) and *Romance* (1903). His literary ambit extends from friendships with Ezra Pound, Wyndham Lewis and H. G. Wells to his American residences and support for writers from Jean Rhys to Hemingway and William Carlos Williams. He vaunts founding editorships of *The English Review* (1908–9) and the one-year-only but highly influential *transatlantic review* (1924). Bloomsbury had its claim on him, as did Paris, New England and the American Midwest. In all he rightly is to be seen helping usher in a new modernist regime of letters, from the Edwardian age to the metropolitan 1920s and into the political 1930s. European literary tradition affords him his admired Flaubert and de Maupassant, along with James and Conrad, and in painting Renoir, Monet, Degas and their generation. His allegiances to the modern were, and remained, essential.

Ford's barb at the Pre-Raphaelites and fellow Victorians as 'the bitter, enormous, greybeard assembly of the Victorian Great' underlines the will forward.[12] He speaks of Victorianism's 'abiding claustrophobia', the freeing of creative impulse represented by the New Novel in particular and by New – Modern – Art in general.[13] Nowhere does this will to modernity achieve greater consequence than in *The Good Soldier*, with its impressionist filtering and uses of indirection. His novel, if not *Ulysses* or 'The Waste Land' or late James, and though it has taken time to win definitive recognition, fully belongs with them in helping create the transition into the varying streams of modernism.

In opening the last part of his account in *The Good Soldier* John Dowell, monied Pennsylvania Quaker and veteran Europe-resident,

104 MODERNS – CHAUCER TO CONTEMPORARY FICTION

puts his narrative credentials into full view. Or Ford would have him appear to do so:

> I have, I am aware, told this story in a very rambling way so that it may be difficult for anyone to find their path through what may be a sort of maze. I cannot help it. I have stuck to my idea of being in a country cottage with a silent listener, hearing between the gusts of wind and amidst the noises of the distant sea, the story as it comes. ... one goes back, one goes forward. One remembers points that one has forgotten and one explains them all the more minutely since one recognizes that one has forgotten to mention them in the proper places and that one may have given, by omitting them, a false impression. (147)

The story Dowell tells, across a pre-World War I transatlantic decade, indeed turns inside out, 'a sort of maze'. Its principals, himself and New England wife Florence, née Hurlbird, the 'perfect' upperclass English couple Captain Edward Ashburnham and Irish-Catholic wife Leonora, and their ward Nancy Rufford, exist as though in two-in-one image.

Geographies shift, the German spa town of Nauheim or English country seat of Branshaw Teleragh, Indian colonial residence or Monte Carlo. But the outward show holds, marriage, class manners, the dinner table, comportment. Under this regime, Victorian in heritage, desire and sublimation always threaten to break through the surface of manners. Ford goes about his business with aplomb, a 'modern' hand, his novel patterned well beyond conventional mystery or thriller. Dowell's assertion of 'rambling', 'omission', going 'back', going 'forward', and perhaps foremost, 'false impression', offers route markers.

The ingenuousness he professes even as suspicion arises of complicity, raises the essential question of trust in him as legatee of 'this story'. 'Well, those are my impressions' (93), he says, recalling his passively arranged marriage with Florence and friendship with the Ashburnhams. Whether or not they are in truth the impressions of a self-declared and colourless American Innocent caught up, and out, by a fallen world, or those of a Janus at every turn implicated in the folds he curates, the novel leaves perfectly in irresolution. Story, if indeed only the one is being told, renders *The Good Soldier* a plausible labyrinth.

The *leitmotif* of good and bad heart plays literally and figuratively into this theatre of deceit. Dowell's celibate marriage to Florence ostensibly saves her from cardiac risk but hides the liaison with Ashburnham, successor to her earlier painter-lover Jimmy, her heart stopped only when she self-poisons with prussic acid. Ashburnham, also the ostensible heart-sufferer, will show gentlemanly open heart to his tenants or the street-needy, and at the same time closed marital heart to Leonora, ready philandering heart to the village girl inside a train carriage, and grievously, to the young married Maisie Maidan who actually dies of heart failure at her disrepute. There follow for him the Spanish dancer-blackmailer, La Dolciquita, and the ward Nancy Rufford, whose breakage at his abandonment leads to her breakdown and final custody with Dowell. The 'good soldier' will arrest his heart in suicide, the open penknife across the throat. For Leonora, as she assumes regulation of Ashburnham, the country seat, and her husband's standing as officer-gentleman despite the affairs, the heart is cold, managerial. Her very Catholic submission to spirit over flesh elides into iron maintenance of the respectable public face of marriage. What tone attaches to Dowell's report of her remarriage to the safe but dull Rodney Bayham, the woman he has thought magnificent and whose husband he professes not just to have admired but loved?

Under Dowell's time-shifts and shards of memory, and always his ambiguous entrances into the action, this 'saddest' story is to be designated 'a record of fatigue' (183), that of 'an ageing American with very little knowledge of life' (190). He bills himself, finally, as 'that absurd figure, an American millionaire' (197), the inheritor of the Ashburnham house and estate, nurse to the catatonic Nancy whom he alleges he loves and whom Leonora has offered to Edward as trophy, and more than all else, literary curator of the contingent relationships that have been his history. Is he the unwitting innocent of his own professed reckoning or more the voyeur? How truly does he admire Edward and Leonora or see in Nancy perfection even as her broken mind reverberates to the word 'shuttlecocks'? What to make of his insouciant reaction to the two suicides? Can credence even be given to the version of him as possible revenger? Ford's modernity in *The Good Soldier* resides as much as anywhere in the resistance to absolute narrator credibility, the un-acceptance of final understandings.

106   MODERNS – CHAUCER TO CONTEMPORARY FICTION

Butler, Strachey, Ford. Their purchase on the modern differs in genre but not animus. They take their aim at assumptions that once governed the Victorian tableau, the public show and, in so doing, explore the altogether more private truth. If not explicitly pulling down the monuments, they disallow the facades of propriety, agreed surfaces. That also means securing appropriate literary forms, or imaginatively repurposing older forms. Whether biography as bio-fiction, history as more than agreed silhouette, or the novel as defiant fiction of fact, the outcome is to put Victorianism and its legacy challengingly under respective versions of the yet newer modern.

Notes

1. For a useful conspectus, see George Levine (ed.), *The Emergence of Victorian Consciousness: The Spirit of the Age*, New York: Collier Macmillan, 1967.
2. References are to the following editions: Samuel Butler, *The Way of All Flesh*, Harmondsworth, Middlesex: Penguin Books, 1947, 1966; Lytton Strachey, *Eminent Victorians*, Harmondsworth, Middlesex: Penguin Books, Revised Edition, 1990; Ford Madox Ford, *The Good Soldier*, Harmondsworth, Middlesex: Penguin Books, 2007.
3. Samuel Butler, *The Notebooks*, London and New York: The Shrewsbury Edition, 1926. Reprinted New York: AMS Press, 1968, 102.
4. Lytton Strachey, *Queen Victoria*, London: Chatto & Windus, 1921.
5. Ford Madox Ford, *Ancient Lights and Certain New Reflections: Being the Memories of a Young Man*, London: Chapman & Hall, 1911.
6. V. S. Pritchett, 'A Victorian Son', *The Living Novel*, London: Chatto & Windus, 1946. Revised and Expanded Edition, *The Living Novel & Later Appreciations*, New York: Random House, 1964, 140–1.
7. Michael Holroyd, *Lytton Strachey: A Biography*, 2 vols, London: William Heinemann, 1967–8. Single volume, Harmondsworth, Middlesex: Viking Penguin, 1971, 1979, 995.
8. R. W. Lid, *Ford Madox Ford: The Essence of His Art*, Berkeley: University of California Press, 1964, 32.
9. E. M. Forster, *Aspects of the Novel*, 1927, 146.
10. William Maxwell, 'Your Affectionate Son', *The Outermost Dream: Essays and Reviews*, New York: Knopf, 1989, 178.
11. Lytton Strachey, *Eminent Victorians*, London: Chatto & Windus, 1918. As indicated, references are to the Penguin edition 1990.
12. Ford Madox Ford, *Portraits from Life, Memories and Criticism*, Boston and New York: Houghton Mifflin Co., 1937, 204.
13. *Portraits from Life, Memories and Criticism*, 22.

CHAPTER 9

Cracked Bells and Intelligent Detonators: The Modern of Conrad's *The Secret Agent*

Spy thriller. The category, for sure, opens the bidding on *The Secret Agent* (1907).[1] Who, on first encounter, would question that Conrad gives every indication of having drawn upon the accepted stock of the genre? A dim Foreign Embassy plan to provoke an English government crack-down on political radicalism ends in a fatally botched bomb attack on the Greenwich Observatory. Verloc as the agent in question, hireling to the Russians and the London metropolitan police alike, causes martyrdom of an innocent and ends up dead by the hand of his wife, herself an eventual suicide in the English Channel. Assorted anarchist types, from pacifist utopians to believers in terror, vie for pride of place – all, by their own word-laden accounts, luminaries of the new kingdom on earth. Arrayed against them stand the guardians of public order, a descending hierarchy of the Minister of State, the Assistant Commissioner, Chief Inspector Heat, and even the bobby who patrols Brett Street where the Verlocs have their Soho shop. As basic terms for this or any other thriller, there would seem few grounds for cavil.

But it takes no long acquaintanceship with *The Secret Agent* to recognise that if Conrad's purpose is thrillerdom, then he has gone about it in ways that might hardly have been anticipated. Everything that plays into the story has been subtly turned inside-out, tacitly subverted. The clandestine meetings, the dutiful talk of revolution, the toings and froings between London and that dire place 'The Continent', the calculations of Mr Vladimir, and even the bomb that takes poor Stevie to his death, amount to an outward show as Conrad projects them, an ever darkening comedy of errors. Suspense applies, but not as the main aim. Whatever the 'plot'

108   MODERNS – CHAUCER TO CONTEMPORARY FICTION

hatched by Verloc's paymasters, or by Sir Ethelred and his subordinates as counter-action, or imprecisely dreamed of by the anarchist ragtag of Karl Yundt, Michaelis, Ossipon and the Professor, it acts as but the shadow of that which engages Conrad overall.

For the plot that truly matters in *The Secret Agent* arises out of Conrad's vision of English society, late Victorian or Edwardian, as one huge collusive dislocation or masquerade. Its endless vaunted composure, cool, pragmatic, understated, indelibly Anglo-Saxon, conceals a kind of shared conspiracy in which surface inexorably and not to say subliminally does duty for substance. And to bring off *this* vision, the far more consequential 'plot', Conrad deploys an irony stronger, and at times more accusing, than anywhere in his fiction, including the South American masterpiece that precedes it, *Nostromo* (1904).

It is to this end that Conrad's novel depicts the English capital as masking behind its daytime face a deeply more sinister and interactive grid. Beset by fog, mud, general murk and shadow, 'a darkness enough to bury five million lives' as he terms it in his Author's Note of 1920, it offers the very image of the metropolis as conspiracy, a city of the hidden and subterranean. Be it thus in insurrectionary quarters, the offices of state, the bureaucracies, the parks, the Soho side-streets, or more to the point, the construct known all too simply as middle-of-the-road England, plotting of one kind or another abounds. The novel seeks nothing less than to encompass their different but interlinking manifestations.

Writing in October 1907 to his friend Cunninghame Graham, who had helped him with Latin American material for *Nostromo*, Conrad himself gave more than a passing indication of his true aims in *The Secret Agent*: 'But I don't think I've been satirizing the revolutionary world. All these people are not revolutionaries – they are shams.'[2] It does not surprise, in this light, that he frequently disavowed any real inside knowledge of the likes of Blanqui, Kropotkin and Bakunin; or of proponents of 'politics by the deed' such as Sergei Nechaev or Peter Tkachev; or of the figure of Martial Bourdin, the historic actual bomber who blew himself to near smithereens in the Greenwich Observatory outrage of February 1894; or of the different Czarist, Marxian and Fenian groups whose activities ran like a political fever through the 1880s and the years immediately following. For Conrad the matter went infinitely deeper than the portrait of mere alarum or sectarian politics. He had in mind, it becomes clear, a far larger moving target, that of London as a paradigm of the human city. To this end the novel gives genuine cause to be associated with the modernity of simulacrum, the matrix in which the unreal co-opts the real.

In this respect his repeated disavowals of Dostoevsky as a factor in the creation of *The Secret Agent* deserve mention. Conrad, as is well enough known, frequently belittled Dostoevsky, accusing him of guilt by association with the imperial Russia which had so often and brutally subjugated his native Poland. This was unfortunate in two ways. It demeaned Conrad in and of itself. More importantly it suggests that he could not fully bring himself to acknowledge how much, directly or otherwise, he owed to works like *Notes from Underground* (1864), *The Idiot* (1969) and *The Devils* (1871–2). For although one can see why Dickens, say, or Zola, or the Turgenev of *Virgin Soil* (1876), have been advanced as influences on *The Secret Agent*, is not Dostoevsky the true fellow-spirit behind the book – the dark, prophetic Dostoevsky of *Crime and Punishment* (1866) and *The Possessed* (1871–2)?

Whatever else, Dostoevsky more than anyone sets up the image of human existence as an 'underground', hell on earth. From this vantage point, also, *The Secret Agent* has frequently led to comparison with Henry James's *The Princess Casamassima* (1886), at one reach psychological drama in the person of Hyacinth Robinson, yet at another, the portrait once again of the modern city as hive or web. Although Conrad's debts may have been several, including those to a number of Scotland Yard memoirs, they finally will not account for the singularity of *The Secret Agent*. For that we need to recognise the kind of imagination at work in the book itself, especially the modern of its use of 'dislocation' in subject, and in every respect as importantly, in narrative fashioning. 'I am *modern*' insisted Conrad, writing in 1902.[3] His novel exactly affords grounds for assigning him imaginative grounds for this stance.

The items alluded to in this chapter's title offer markers for the 'manner of presenting' the novel as a whole. Consider, first, the cracked bell. Conrad begins *The Secret Agent* on a note of seeming impeccable realism. Verloc steps out from the shop, leaving it in the care of his brother-in-law with Mrs Verloc as back-up. The shop appears almost insistently ordinary, familiar. Have we not before us that most English of institutions, the residential small family business? But anomalies quickly press for attention. Why is Verloc's business done at night for the most part? Why does he care 'but little about his ostensible business' (46)? What else lies within this 'grimy' 'square' house and shop (46)? As the scene builds, Conrad effortlessly causes the focus to tilt. This is not in effect realism, but things caught obliquely, at a slight but deliberate miscued angle. A first and necessary dislocation has taken place, a dissimulative screen, one in the many to follow.

'In the daytime the door remained closed; in the evening it stood discreetly but suspiciously ajar' (45). Verloc's shop may indeed look like a place of respectable commerce, but its traffic has to do with buying and selling by stealth, the surreptitious clink of coins and no questions asked. Here, the emporium's forlorn pornography and supposed radicalism play a crucial role. Shoddy in themselves, they also suggest the shoddiness of lives lived on counterfeit terms – those of manufactured sexual fantasy, hopelessly schismatic politics. So is to be inferred from Conrad's inventory, 'French' dirty-book publications, the 'dingy' (45) casket of charcoal, the dusty inks and stamps and the like, and the obscure and ill-printed journals mock-triumphally trading as *Torch* and *Gong*. A name like *Gong*, especially, offers implicit parody of whatever imagined apocalypse might be thought to beckon. And it also points forward to the Verloc bell.

Casting a shadow over the shop are the gas jets, 'turned low' (45), their sanctioning half-light meant 'either for economy's sake or for the sake of the customers' (45). As to the latter a sorrier parade would be hard to imagine. Young men pass in and out bent upon their off-colour purchases often comically caught out by having to buy from Mrs Verloc. Their elder counterparts, usually in threadbare clothes, muddied, their coats tight about them, equally turn desire on its head. They 'dodge' into the shop 'sideways', 'fidgety' and 'one shoulder down' (45). Step for step the pastiche not only captures things through a glass darkly but through a glass which distorts or dislocates in the consummate right degree.

The bell, however, most completes the picture, a bell Verloc's column of 'customers' are 'afraid to start' (46) lest it draw attention to their furtive purchases.

THE MODERN OF CONRAD'S *THE SECRET AGENT*   111

The bell, hung on the door by means of a curved ribbon of steel, was difficult to circumvent. It was hopelessly cracked; but of an evening, at the slightest provocation, it clattered behind the customer with impudent virulence. (46)

Aptly as 'hopelessly cracked' reflects on Verloc's commercial clientele, it typically also does larger service. It speaks to the society Conrad imagines overall. Is Sir Ethelred, for instance, any less 'cracked' than the would-be politicos who troop in and out of Verloc's parlour? Or the Assistant Commissioner with his allusions to playing Big Game Hunter, than The Professor who threatens mutual destruction by dynamite of anyone who gets too close? Or Verloc himself, who, if he indeed purveys 'shady wares', be they sexual, political, or even his dubious displays of marital responsibility, does so in the guise of upstanding paterfamilias and tradesman?

Conrad, further, invites recognition of what is implied by the accompanying lexicon of 'clattered', 'cracked' and 'virulence'. For ahead will lie the bomb and Stevie's fate, scenes like his poignant but almost fantastical cab-ride down to the south London almshouse, Winnie's spirals of despair, and the double violence of Verloc's and her own death. Graphic as each is, paining to a fault, they become the more so by Conrad's version of each pictured as though belonging to collusive charade, dislocated theatre. The bell 'clatters', accordingly, at frequent intervals, but most of all at key moments of change.

It does so the night before Verloc leaves on one of his clandestine missions to the Continent and as he contemplates a coming change of regime on account of Vladimir's summons to duty. It does so before his mother-in-law's removal. It does so at the dinner table when Verloc looks upon his wife with desire and she asks Stevie to stop shuffling his feet. It does so when Verloc is surprised by the arrival of the anarchist fugitive. It does so when Heat arrives shortly afterwards in hopes of questioning him. It does so again, and even more portentously, when Heat confers with Verloc and is overheard by Winnie. An absolute last time it is to be heard on Winnie's departure with Ossipon after the murder of Verloc ('The cracked bell clattered behind the closed door in the empty shop', 256). This accumulation of sound, tinny, liminally situated, carries dislocation at its every jarring. In each case 'the aggressive clatter of the bell' (198) sounds for the yet profounder dislocation being signalled, the toll as it might be thought of each successive lurch into the abyss.

In like manner, The Professor's detonator provides the terms for another round of dislocation. 'To deal with a man like me', The Professor tells Ossipon as more than a touch discrepantly they go about the all too ordinary business of supping beer, 'you require sheer, naked, inglorious heroism' (91). He speaks as the ranking anarch, the ex-laboratory assistant who has elevated himself into a human time bomb. To this end, he carries in his pocket the onanistic 'indiarubber ball' (91) which when squeezed will ignite on a delay of twenty seconds an explosion of magnum force. Conrad, however, resists the temptation to turn him into simple caricature, a cloak-and-dagger or nitroglycerine-carrying figure out of melodrama. Obsessional, absolutist he may be, but he also operates out of an undeniable if unlovely logic. Indeed, Conrad scarcely covers up a certain relish of The Professor's adversarial urge to pull down the whole house of English life and society. Nor can it be thought less than a stroke of genius to have The Professor, one of the fraternity's own, berate his fellow anarchists. Karl Yunt he mocks as a 'posturing shadow' (93). Ossipon and the other he thinks self-incriminatingly 'talk, print, and do nothing' (96). Verloc, who has made fiasco out of the Greenwich bombing, is said in sternest condemnation to require a 'disclaimer' (100).

However plausible in these aspects, Conrad endows The Professor with yet others which show him to have tilted far off-balance. Born of 'a delicate dark enthusiast' (102) father, an adherent 'of some obscure but rigid Christian sect' (102), he has given way to 'a frenzied puritanism of ambition' (102), the messianic duty of destroying law and institutions in the cause of new justice. That we also learn he is 'lost in the crowd, miserable and undersized' (102), helps explain his compensating resort to the indiarubber ball and all it portends ('the supreme guarantee of his sinister freedom', 102). The Professor, in other words, typifies idealism that kills, the Grand Design gone askew.

His very appearance gives support. He has eyelids that snap 'nervously' (60), a 'sallow' face (90), spectacles like 'unwinking orbs flashing a cold fire' (90) and 'thin vivid lips' (90). He wears suitably meagre clothes of 'nondescript brown' (91), at once 'threadbare' and 'dusty' (91) and marked by 'ragged' buttonholes (91). The tube, just visible, which connects the rubber ball to the sinister flask, suggests 'a slender brown worm' (91). To complete matters, The Professor discloses with exactly the right, but suspect, high seriousness the great challenge of his life:

> I am trying to invent a detonator that would adjust itself to all conditions of action, and even to unexpected changes of conditions. A variable and yet perfectly precise mechanism. A really intelligent detonator. (92)

Yet if in one way odd, even comic, the implications of The Professor's search for his detonator are not lost on Ossipon, especially not when, over a further round of drinks, The Professor boasts were his bomb to go off there and then 'nobody in this room could hope to escape' (92). Even Ossipon, the robust philanderer, the ex-medical student who enjoys the sobriquet of 'The Doctor', finds his nerves jangled. He conjures up 'a dreadful black hole belching horrible fumes', 'smashed brickwork' and 'mutilated corpses' (92). Ossipon, viscerally, dislocatedly, has registered the true import of The Professor's ferocious preconditions for the new society.

The detonator localises all of this. In The Professor's scheme it recurs like an incantation: not only the 'really intelligent detonator' but the 'perfect detonator' (93), the 'really dependable detonator' (97) and 'the absolutely foolproof detonator' (99). Through its means The Professor as 'moral agent' (102) will engage in authentic terrorism, the final, literally explosive overthrow of 'the immense multitude' (103). That his search for the right detonator links to the one which has obliterated Stevie, or Verloc as he mistakenly thinks, can be of no consequence for him. He honours only his own inner dictates of 'a new concept of life' (107), 'a clean sweep and a clear start' (97). Driven, hater of crowds, this would-be usher of the new millennium stalks the streets of London muttering and with the gleam of private revolution in his eye. Dislocated himself, he seeks to dislocate all about him – subject, such is Conrad's sardonic vision, to the appropriate 'sudden hole in time and place' (105) and, lest we forget, his 'really intelligent detonator'.

114   MODERNS – CHAUCER TO CONTEMPORARY FICTION

Bell and detonator typify the dislocation that Conrad portrays as the condition of things in *The Secret Agent*. Other features, equally symptomatic, recur, all of them made to gather in resonance as the narrative takes its course. One has the circles drawn by Stevie (50), the image of an English world turning endlessly on its provincial axis. Verloc's hat typifies the creature of habit, even apathy, rather than some disturber of the peace. Michaelis's obesity, that of a ticket-of-leave jailbird to be sure but also of an overweight child, implies a dreamer funded by his lady patron rather than a fighting social-ist. Ethelred's 'Be concise' becomes the catchphrase of a gloriously out-of-touch Whitehall mandarin more concerned with the fisher-ies than political violence. To add to the list, Conrad emphasises Chief Inspector Heat's search-and arrest mentality which equates politics with lawbreaking and anarchism with burglary; the fatal carving knife which steers between metaphor (the stab in the back for Verloc by Vladimir) and fact (the literal cutlery used by Verloc for his last meal and as the murder weapon); and the misnumber-ing of the London houses so unperturbedly accepted as normal by Verloc as he makes his way from Brett Street to the Embassy. None assumes undue pride of place but belong inside the novel's cata-logue of things finely off-centre, a modernly told off-centreness that permeates each major sequence and relationship.

When, at the outset, Verloc steps out from his shop he steps out from a domestic set-up not so much eccentric as just out of focus with itself. Verloc himself has 'an air of having wallowed, fully dressed, all day on an unmade bed' (46). Mrs Verloc, Winnie, for all the implied sexual vitality of her 'youth' (46) and 'full, rounded form' (47), gives off an 'unfathomable reserve' (47). Both Verlocs, indeed, might be said to live at an agreed one emotional reserve from the other, partners in the deal struck over Stevie rather than any authentic marital intimacy or love. Winnie's mother, legs swollen, more heart than head, belongs in their menagerie as part of the 'furniture' (47). As for Stevie, his dislocation lies in what he is biologically, retarded but benign, one of Nature's Innocents. He registers the world, not unlike William Faulkner's Benjy in *The Sound and The Fury*, only by the evidence of his nerves and senses. His eventual victimry, blown to nothing except for his name-tag, brutally completes all that has gone before. The list includes lack of memory for messages, alarm at stray animals, distraction at 'the comedies of the streets' (49), panic at fallen horses and, above

THE MODERN OF CONRAD'S *THE SECRET AGENT*   115

all, frenzy at the sight and sound of fireworks. In the spectrum of London, from Ethelred to The Professor, assumed good order, Stevie becomes the almost inevitable casualty.

Certainly it is as servant more of order than unorder that Verloc makes his way to Vladimir. 'Bloodshot' (51) may be the sun that shines over the capital, yet the aspects which win Verloc's approval are those of 'opulence and luxury' (51), the 'hygienic' display of high bourgeois English life (52). Nor, even more of note, does Verloc propose the slightest disruption of this state. To the contrary, he is devoted to it with a sort of 'inert fanaticism' (52) which Conrad also inverts into 'fanatical inertness' (52). Were we not to know better, and despite his French mother, Verloc would pass as exemplary Little Englander. His mission, however, against his best instincts, has exactly to do with the end of his *socialiste de salon* posture. 'Inert', 'undemonstrative', 'steady' (52), as Conrad's deflationary irony terms him, Verloc must do that most un-English thing: take action.

The signs turn ominous. Number 10, Chesham Square, stands between Numbers 9 and 37. 'What is desired', announces Wurmt, the lugubrious Chancelier d'Ambassade whose trade is exactly words not action, 'is the occurrence of something definite' (55), 'an alarming fact' (56) to bring down the arm of English authority in line with Czarist reaction to dissidence. Wurmt notes Verloc's corpulence, the obverse of expected weight for an agent in the field. On confronting Vladimir, Verloc hears a First Secretary wholly out of keeping with his 'drawing-room reputation as an agreeable and entertaining man' (57). Verloc has bumbled plots in the past; is now too fat even to fall for some *femme fatale*; is accused of taking money under false pretences; lacks an education in Latin; and in the unkindest cut of all, is to be mocked for having been given star billing since the time of 'the late Baron Stott-Wartenheim' as 'the celebrated agent Δ'(63).

Just as Vladimir can switch accents and languages at will, so Verloc comes over as counterfeit anarchist out of bed too early and the supplier of information simply contemptible to his paymaster. His 'confounded nonsense' (69) completes itself for Vladimir in the fact that he is married, yet another break with anarchist style. Little wonder that Conrad directs attention to London's 'rusty sunshine' (62) and 'the first fly of the year' (62) as sardonically appropriate harbingers of Spring and of 'the jolly good scare' (64) which will be the bomb attack on the Greenwich Observatory. Even Verloc's 'providential' (72) marriage to Winnie, as her mother refers to it, takes on darker implication; this will be providence truly disastrous. Dislocation has again found its working idiom, Conrad's prowess as modern storyteller.

The Verlocs and the anarchists are not alone in coming under Conrad's regime of modern refractions and mirrors. Sir Ethelred, the Assistant Commissioner and Heat as the three exemplars of English public officialdom are done in exactly matching idiom, again, well to the right side of caricature yet subtly awry. Each, credibly, holds an office of consequence: Cabinet Minister, police second-in-command at the London Met, 'operational detective'. Conrad portrays them again as just off-centre, and off-centre, it can be added, in a very English sort of way. For though they hold real power in a real London, they also have given way to a dislocation in their make-up. They appear always slightly out of sync, the inhabitants of silhouette no less than Verloc, Vladimir, The Professor and the rest. They role-play themselves as it were. Their shared dislocation again puts Conrad's reader on familiar ground.

Sir Ethelred is met through his secretary, the Dickensian Toodles. Where Vladimir's Wurmt is all in black, bald and 'with a mincing step' (54), Toodles has 'symmetrically arranged hair' (141) and the look 'of a large and neat schoolboy' (141). That inverse parallel established, so, equally, is that of Ethelred with Vladimir, both men high in their self-esteem and both political actor-managers. For Ethelred, Conrad does a portrait in magnification:

> Vast in bulk and suture, with a long white face, which, broadened at the base by a big double chin, appeared egg-shaped in the fringe of grayish whisker, the great personage seemed an expanding man. Unfortunate from a tailoring point of view, the crossfolds in the middle of a buttoned black coat added to the impression, as if the fastenings of the garment were tried to the utmost. From the head, set upward on a thick neck, the eyes, with puffy lower lids, stared with a haughty droop on each side of a hooked, aggressive nose, nobly salient in the vast pale circumference of the face. A shiny silk hat and a pair of worn gloves lying ready at the end of a long table looked expanded, too, enormous. (142)

Rarely can the born-to-rule mandarin have been better caught. Inflated in body and couture, Sir Ethelred gives the very reflection of upper-class English insouciance. And that, Conrad takes upon himself to confirm in the run of catchphrases put before the Assistant Commissioner in his interview about the Greenwich explosion. 'Don't go into details. I have no time for that' (142), he insists, to be followed in turn by 'Spare me the details' (143), 'No need to go into details' (143) and 'Be as concise as you can' (146). He speaks, as it were, mirror jargon, upper echelon and mystificatory in its own way as anything spoken by the anarchists.

As to the Assistant Commissioner, he could well be in the wrong country, the ex-colonial officer who patrols the English capital as though set down in some unexpected part of the Empire. His dislocation has the familiar ring of the servant of the crown who finds he has no real knowledge of the crown he serves, the outsider suddenly on the inside. His commutes between Sir Ethelred's office and the Verloc shop, between Heat and The Professor, situate him as oddly out of joint with his mission, less master than servant of the situation.

Equally so Inspector Heat. Even less than the Assistant Commissioner does he perceive what is at stake in the Greenwich affair. For him this is all police procedure, a crime committed, suspects to be arrested, reports to be filed. He grasps nothing of the moral calamity at the heart of what has happened, nor the different kinds of sham and ineptitude that have led to Stevie's death. As the details emerge, Ethelred understands that something 'very fantastic' (202) has occurred. The Assistant Commissioner discerns 'a ferocious joke' (202). Heat, too close to events, can only pay Verloc 'a friendly call' (192), and in a supreme irony as he goes about 'regulation' inquiries cause Winnie to overhear and so bring down the final curtain on the drama. Neither Sir Ethelred, nor the Assistant Commissioner, nor Heat, in other words, grasps the whole. Conrad's feat is to allow his reader full entrance into the storyline while at the same time inviting recognition that the one storyline binds the other, the torque of modern narration.

If Conrad's 'ironic method' (41) applies to *The Secret Agent* as spy or political thriller, it assuredly does so as 'a domestic drama' (204), in the Assistant Commissioner's phrase to Sir Ethelred. The Verlocs are offered as a counterfeit marriage at one with the goods they sell.

118   MODERNS – CHAUCER TO CONTEMPORARY FICTION

They typify the pairing that has settled for less. Winnie has foregone her young butcher, married Verloc to her mother's uncomprehending approval in order to protect Stevie, and fondly and mistakenly come to think Verloc and Stevie the image of father and son. Conrad shows them actually to be a family becoming un-familial, self-prostituted as the kind of London in which they find themselves situated. The evidence further accumulates in the removal of Winnie's mother to the almshouse south of the river, and then in the final, momentous dislocation of Verloc's death and Winnie's suicide.

First there is the mother-in-law's conception of what she is doing, handing over means and property to both her children and Verloc ('a sensible union with that excellent husband', 156). But the cabby who comes to bring her resembles a gargoyle ('His enormous and unwashed countenance flamed red in the muddy stretch of the street', 157). The journey down Whitehall veers into a gradient which causes 'time itself . . . to stand still' (157). For Stevie, it is the whip on the horse which arouses his over-excitability – the cabby having dilated into the Devil with the boy his spellbound victim. As they wend their way through London as City of Dreadful Night ('dirty', 'noisy', 'hopeless', 'rowdy', 159), the old lady is moved to tears at the thought of Mr Verloc's 'excellence' (159), his role of family protector. She could not be more adrift. The inversions are those of dark masquerade.

When, en route, the 'night cabby' (165) whose 'decayed clothing' (164) and diatribe on being cold and hungry, without a fare, and beset by drunks, works its effect upon the impressionable Stevie, it becomes the completion of a journey by 'the Cab of Death' (167). London, literal-seeming London, is evidently to hand. Through Stevie it transposes into a psychic trench, whose surfaces hide pain, grief, farce and tragedy. The dislocation Stevie internalises in the thought of the horse's being lame and the cabman's wait for fares until two in the morning. His summary word is 'dread' (164). Nor does Stevie fail to note that the cabman touches him with an 'iron hook' which protrudes from 'a raggedy, greasy sleeve' (164). The cabman, in turn, summarises his respective distress in seeking to provide for a wife and four children in the understatement 'This ain't an easy world' (165). Conrad has the journey, the horse, the cabman and his family, and impending loss of his own mother, compete for primacy in Stevie's 'sensations' (165). He speaks the one gloss – 'Bad! Bad!' (165). It speaks worlds.

THE MODERN OF CONRAD'S *THE SECRET AGENT*   119

Stevie's broken phrases, his instinctive vocabulary of dislocation, do not stop there. 'Poor brute' (168) he says of the horse to his sister. 'Poor! Poor!' (168) he repeats as Winnie deposits their mother. His staccato utterances build one upon the other until they resemble a set of antistrophes. Whatever may posture as the myth of a benign 'condition of England', for Stevie the condition signifies hurt and fracture, poverty amid wealth, hollowness. The paradox of his flawed but actually consummate articulacy gives emphasis:

> The docile Stevie went along; but now he went along without pride, shamblingly, and muttering half words, and even words that would have been whole if they had not been made up of halves that did not belong to each other. It was as though he had been trying to fit all the words he could remember to his sentiments in order to get some sort of corresponding idea. And as a matter of fact, he got it at last. He hung back to utter it at once. 'Bad world for poor people'. (168)

'Halves that did not belong to each other' applies in the immediate instance to Stevie's speech habits. But it equally applies to the society about him. The Verlocs have married only to lead emotionally separate lives. The politicos, whether establishment or anarchist, as much split one against the other as across the political divide. Sir Ethelred works at a distance from his Assistant Commissioner, as does he in turn from his Chief Inspector. London may vaunt itself a hub of empire, an England forever unitedly and contentedly England, but it harbours pervasive ravines and cracks. Stevie, Conrad's damaged human barometer, gives the appropriate graph.

Winnie's decline and fall stretches across the final chapters, beginning from her 'acute pang of loneliness' (173) at her mother's removal. Conrad locates her within 'modern' time metaphors. She hears the 'lonely' clock tick towards 'the abyss of eternity' (175). As she and Verloc lie side by side the light she extinguishes becomes the perfect curtain for the darkness between them. Verloc's trip to the Continent, top spy, comes under Conrad's mock-heroic imagery, Odysseus to Penelope (176). The accent falls, calculatedly, upon Verloc's doings, *his* importance, *his* view of life, *his* view of his wife as marital property, *his* interview with Heat, and *his* estimate of Vladimir as 'Hyperborean swine' (198). Conrad situates these exhalations against Winnie's deafening silence, and more than anything

120   MODERNS – CHAUCER TO CONTEMPORARY FICTION

against her reaction to the literally un-sayable destruction of Stevie. She has only the label from her brother's coat, his remnant. Heat's description appals:

> Blown to small bits: limbs, gravel, clothing, bones, splinters – all mixed together. I tell you they had to fetch a shovel to gather him up with. (196)

Winnie's reaction of catatonia (she is said to be 'immobile', 198) is given yet greater force as she looks upon the mock-glimmer of her wedding ring (198). She too has become the very figure of dislocation, sister, daughter, wife, widow, murderer, fugitive. No surprise that Conrad has the bell give its final clatter.

Verloc, meanwhile, is allowed to continue his sublime egotism. '"I didn't mean any harm to come to the boy"' (211) runs his apology to Winnie as though Stevie were merely injured or exposed to some passing ailment. The augmenting insistence of his 'apology' in not taking better care contrasts utterly with her refusal to use words. Detail becomes ironic commentary: the carving knife and fork which Verloc uses to eat his cold beef and bread; the home he now thinks will become a 'prison' for a while; the Brett Street parlour as a 'cage'; and Winnie's rising perception that 'freedom' lies in plunging the knife into her husband's body. The more her grim, lost and infinitely sad recognition grows, the more Verloc talks on – of his pride in being part of 'every murdering plot for the last eleven years' (217), of his own outrage at the inconvenience of Stevie's death, of his powers to have wooed and bedded Winnie. The gap becomes grotesque, black. And in knifing Verloc, Conrad has her become a tableau both ancient and modern, the parody of solicitous wife gazing upon her lost beloved.

For her flight, having re-met Ossipon and with the doorbell clattering its closing toll, the description again enacts charade, that of romantic escape:

> Winnie Verloc turning about held him by both arms, facing him under the falling mist in the darkness and solitude of Brett Place, in which all sounds of life seemed lost as if in a triangular well of asphalt and bricks, of blind houses and unfeeling stones. (244)

No more than Verloc can Ossipan grasp what has passed through Winnie, her trauma both as Stevie's sister and destiny as unexpected avenger. It falls to him, too, to offer the last dislocated picture of Verloc, prince of spies:

> Night, the inevitable reward of men's faithful labours on this earth, night had fallen on Mr Verloc, the tried revolutionist – 'one of the old lot' – the humble guardian of society; the invaluable secret agent Δ of Baron Stott-Wartenheim's dispatches, a servant of law and order, faithful, trusted, accurate, admirable, with perhaps one singe amiable weakness: the idealistic belief in being loved for himself. (252)

Winnie knows better. But her fear of the fourteen-foot drop in being hanged, her hysteria, unmans even the self-vauntingly 'robust' Ossipon. His jump from the train as it leaves the station, the womaniser mocked and the inheritor of Verloc's cash but not his wife, acts as supreme parody of the lover's leap, one more silhouette folded into life. Only the waters of the English Channel await Winnie, her long day's journey into night completed. Conrad has his novel find its epitaph in The Professor, his thoughts 'like a pest' (269) turned to 'images of ruin and destruction' (269). Conrad bequeaths one final turn of the screw, one final image of a modern world caught in dislocation.

A century or more on from the publication of *The Secret Agent*, western 'modernity' has become increasingly familiar with suicide terrorism, be it 9-11 or the London, Paris and other attacks across Europe. Conrad's novel, on occasion, has been invoked for its prescience. But that is to transpose a work of narrative imagination into political playbook, a species of news media. The modern resides in the manner in which the event at its centre is assumed into the author's very idiom, the organising style of disclosure. For that we have Conrad himself:

> After all I am a writer of fiction, and it is not what actually happens, but the manner of presenting it that settles the literary and even moral value of my work.[4]

MODERNS – CHAUCER TO CONTEMPORARY FICTION

The novel's rhythm of contingent opposites and refractions, its mirror irony, captures perspectivally the dislocation enacted within its plot line. In this respect, and with unique display, Conrad conveys his lasting possession of the modern.

Notes

1. Joseph Conrad, *The Secret Agent*, London: J. M. Dent & Sons, 1907. Page references throughout are to *The Secret Agent*, Harmondsworth, Middlesex: Penguin, 1963, reprinted as a Penguin Classic, 1986, 1987, 1988. I am indebted to a number of major studies of Conrad, the following more so than others: F. R. Leavis, *The Great Tradition*, London: Chatto & Windus, 1948; Irving Howe, *Politics and the Novel*, Cleveland, OH: Meridian Books, 1957; E. M. Tillyard, 'The Secret Agent Reconsidered', *Essays in Criticism*, XI, 3, July 1961, 303–18; H. M. Daleski, *Joseph Conrad: The Way of Dispossession*, London: Faber & Faber, 1977: Jacques Berthoud, *Joseph Conrad: The Major Phase*, Cambridge: Cambridge University Press, 1978; and Daniel R. Schwartz, *Conrad: Almayer's Folly to Under Western Eyes*, London: Macmillan, 1980.
2. Frederick R. Karl and Laurence Davies (eds), *The Collected Letters of Joseph Conrad*, Vol. 3, 1903–7, Cambridge: Cambridge University Press, 1988. Conrad to R. B. Cunninghame Graham, 7 October 1907, 491.
3. See Leo Robson, 'Conrad's Journey', *The New Yorker*, November 2017.
4. Joseph Conrad to Alfred Thomas Saunders, 14 June 1917.

CHAPTER 10

Women's Modern: Mina Loy, Dorothy Richardson, Jean Rhys

Almost of necessity one begins from Virginia Woolf, her output, her life, and nowhere more so than in *A Room of One's Own* (1928):

> Like most uneducated Englishwomen – I like reading books in the bulk. Lately my diet has become a trifle monotonous; history is too much about wars, biography too much about great men; poetry has shown, I think, a tendency to sterility, and fiction – but I have sufficiently exposed my disabilities as a critic of modern fiction and will say no more about it. Therefore I would ask you to write all kinds of books, hesitating at no subject however trivial or however vast.[1]

This address to authorship and women flags her tenacity: novelist, essay writer, feminist, essential Bloomsbury spirit, and co-founder of the Hogarth Press with Leonard Woolf. In the face of the patriarchy of her Victorian scholar father Sir Leslie Stephen, the prowess as painter of her elder sibling Vanessa Bell, and male family sexual pestering, she was able to establish autonomous terms and conditions. Her lived-out bisexuality, notably reflected in the relationship with both Leonard and Vita Sackville-West, anticipates latter-day challenges to sexual boundary. The notorious depressive episodes, and suicide, associate her with a line that leads on to Sylvia Plath, Anne Sexton and Ann Quin. Fracture, eventually, doomed her in life, but she takes her place as no ready martyr – rather the exceptional experimentalist, a confident doyenne.

Like Joyce she helps shape the modern novel into the modernist novel, her interest in narrative forms of story part of the larger movement that assumes European scale as to self-conscious experiments of assemblage and memory. The novels she began with *The Voyage*

123

Out (1915), and continued through *Mrs. Dalloway* (1925), *To the Lighthouse* (1927), *The Waves* (1931) and *Between the Acts* (1941), however often interpretation locks them into stream of consciousness cliché, achieve unique flourish of antiphonal voice, associative image. *Between the Acts* concentrates Woolf's fictional practices overall, the *compte rendu* of her views on gender, war, self and community. *Three Guineas* (1938), essay-sequel to *A Room of One's Own*, adds thinking about compositional theory to her credential as modernist. None of which overlooks lingering cavils about aestheticism, or well-heeled class hauteur and casual anti-Semitism.

The call for 'all kinds of books' by women resonates across the board, whether for her own time or ahead, and those especially to be written under different kinds of 'modern' canopy. Exemplarily they find expression in Mina Loy's imagist mosaics of the *Lunar Baedeker* verse collections (1923, 1958), Dorothy Richardson's Pilgrimage saga launched with *Pointed Roofs* (1915), and Jean Rhys's Caribbean-Atlantic novel *Wide Sargasso Sea* (1966).

Their corridors into the workings of gender, and women's autonomy or its lack, take on evident historic importance. But so, in equal measure, do the regimes of verse- and novel-writing that give these issues their imaginative bearing. The modes of composition on offer, whether poem as collage, or threaded female saga, or inspired postcolonial intertext, position their authors alongside Woolf in also bringing the modern into the modernist, a kind of twentieth-century ultra gallery of the modern.

The degree to which Mina Loy (1882–1966) is granted English literary standing inevitably arises. Birth, certainly, begins in London, to a Hungarian Jewish father and Christian-evangelical mother. Her art years in Munich, Berlin, Florence, Paris and New York see the name-change from Mina Gertrude Löwry to Mina Loy. Loy the writer co-exists with the visual and line-graphic artist, oil painter, sculptor, assemblage-maker and lampshade designer. The United States which becomes her eventual residence and citizenship has her based from 1916 through to her death successively in New York's Bowery and in Colorado. It was a life, across geographies, tied into the avant-garde and over time to number among her great friendships and influences Gertrude Stein, Isadora Duncan, Ezra Pound,

Marcel Duchamp, Djuna Barnes, Carl Van Vechten and Man Ray. Her contribution, still to arrive at full recognition, places her in the forward tiers of the transatlantic creative modern.

Loy's literary output crosses genres, the poetry of the *Lunar Baedeker* collections, to include the thirty-four untitled anti-romance 'love' sequence 'Songs to Joannes', her posthumous novel *Insel* (1981) and *Stories and Essays* (2011).[2] 'Feminist Manifesto', reprinted in *Lunar Baedeker*, its wording variously underlined or printed in bold, sets out her uncompromising New Woman beliefs. Men and women are forever locked in a circling power-contest, for the most part predatory and un-resolvable. Sex, the act of, offers momentary reprise, but little else:

> Men & women are enemies, with the enmity of the exploited for the parasite . . . the only point at which the interests of the sexes merge – is the sexual embrace.[3]

In a single-line poem, whose concision (and typography) recalls her greatly favoured Emily Dickinson, she offers a cryptic reflexive summary:

> Love – – – the preeminent litterateur
> ('Song to Joannes' XXXI, 68)

The poetry, especially its take on men–women relationship as irretrievably embattled, has understandably most come to avail, key in localising her modern credential.

Poems as elliptical, not to say religio-sexual, as one of the opening pieces in 'Songs to Joannes' (III) further suggests why this has been the case:

> We might have coupled
> In the bed-ridden monopoly of a moment
> Or broken flesh with one another
> At the profane communion table
> Where wine is spill'd on promiscuous lips
> We might have given birth to a butterfly
> With the daily-news
> Printed in blood on its wings. (54)

126   MODERNS – CHAUCER TO CONTEMPORARY FICTION

What to speculate of the 'might have' been follow-on to the given encounter, the coupling, bed, flesh, drink, lips, left-over fantasy? 'Profane communion table' sets the note of disenchantment, the imagery again obligingly sardonic.

'Parturition' (4–8), one of Loy's longer pieces in 'Songs to Joannes', takes another un-sacral view, birth-giving not as celebration but the process in which 'I am the centre/ Of a circle of pain/ Exceeding its boundaries in every direction'. Sensations arise of 'nerve vibration' and 'contraction'. Fantasy 'nice' girl-ditty intrudes. The blur of a 'distorted mountain of agony' hovers. Lost 'repose' becomes all. 'Emptying of life' co-exists with 'giving life' to herself even as her lover absconds upstairs to another woman. Has not the new mother, the poem asks, become in a near-surreal image the hybrid insect-bird, a 'deadwhite feathered moth/ Laying eggs'?

She may now belong to 'infinite Maternity' and 'cosmic reproductivity', but the experience has created the 'subconscious/ Impression of a cat/ With blind kittens/ Among her legs'. 'I am that cat', she alleges, the wearer of a 'ludicrous little halo' as though mock Madonna. The closing lines, elliptical as always, show no hosanna to birth:

> I once heard in a church
> – Man and woman God made the them
> Thank God (8)

God's act of childbirth, Adam and Eve ('the them'), on this measure has not caused birth-pangs like her own, nothing if not feminist-modern taunt on Loy's part.

These tight-strung formulations of disjuncture between men and women run through almost all the output. 'Songs to Joannes' virtually thrives on them, a soliloquy in serial her equivalent of T. S. Eliot's 'The Love Song of J. Alfred Prufrock'. To capture the sourness of love promised and then unstrung or punitive, Loy has words bracket surreally, antonyms join unexpectedly. Spacing, the indentation and hyphens deployed as deliberate verse geometry, reflects split and remorse. Two sequences offer examples:

> XII
> Voices break on the confines of passion
> Desire Suspicion Man Woman
> Solve in the humid carnage (57)

XIV
Today
Everlasting passing apparent imperceptible
To you
I bring the nascent virginity of
—Myself for the moment (58)

The effect is a kind of emotional colour-field of pained accusation, the irregularity of phrase duly apt.

'Lunar Baedecker' (81–2), the title-poem, exhibits Loy's poetic lens at characteristically oblique angle. The view is expansive, the wax and wane of love's illusion ('the flight/ of Eros obsolete'), the romantic moon's deception ('the fossil virgin of the skies'). 'Apology of Genius' (77–8) undermines perennial human pretension ('We are the sacerdotal clowns/ who feed upon the wind and stars'). 'Letters of the Unliving' (129–32) mourns a dead husband ('Can one who still has being/ be inexistent?'), the poem to be understood as her 'calligraphy of recollection'. The speaker endures 'memory's languor', self-identifying as 'an older Ophelia/ on Lethe'. Loy's sleights perhaps too often verge towards the overwrought, the extravagant torque. Her versions of the modern, vision and form, can fairly be said not to come without test or price. But read in good faith they greatly repay expenditure.

The full sweep of Dorothy Richardson's Pilgrimage novels, *Pointed Roofs* (1915) to *March Moonlight* (post. 1967), bespeaks long haul on her part and challenge to sustained attention for her readership. Despite publisher confidence in her writing (Duckworth in the UK, Knopf in the USA), the several collected editions (1936, 1967, 1979) and the gather of critical scholarship, this show of multi-volume length has tended to undercut her better impact. Complaints attach to the over-particularity of detail, crowdedness within smallness of circuit. Fortunately, not unusual with *roman fleuve* as in the case of Proust, other dimensions summon attention. The accumulating fictional biography of her alter ego, Miriam Henderson, which Richardson memorably spoke of as 'chapters' in one ongoing composite novel, marks equally her attempt to create a discernible women's styling of narrative – viewpoint, detail, tone.[4]

The approach becomes evident from the start. Richardson stays in the third person but positions Miriam always centripetally, both

128   MODERNS – CHAUCER TO CONTEMPORARY FICTION

actor in her own history and evolving monitor of its implications. The story that begins with seventeen-year-old Miriam's move from comfortable late-Victorian England to German finishing school as language teacher in *Pointed Roofs* and eventually into the vexed intimacy of adult relationship with both men and women in *Dawn's Left Hand* (1931), *Clear Horizon* (1935) and the posthumous *March Moonlight*, acts as a life-graph, Miriam and her evolving reflection in the mirror.

The increments build, governess in *Backwater* (1916) and *Honeycomb* (1917), dental receptionist in *The Tunnel* (1919), everyday tenant in *Interim* (1920), aspirant philosophic thinker in *Deadlock* (1921), and friend and lover in *Revolving Lights* (1923), *The Trap* (1925) and *Oberland* (1928). Centred for the most part in London, these 'chapter' novels thread into the single tapestry of female consciousness, wholly immediate worlds of event or experience yet audited at every stage by Miriam herself. Richardson, who dismissed attributions of stream of consciousness, nonetheless has her storytelling converge into this one presiding modernity of voice.

Painted Roofs not only inaugurates the unfolding interactions in the life of Miriam Henderson, but does so as specimen kind of narrative for the entire Pilgrimage collection. Amid the orbit first of well-heeled Home Counties parents and sisters, then the girl pupils under the tutelage of the austere Fräulein Pfaff in Germany, she begins to take stock of herself as emerging identity. The German ambit unremittingly reflects genteel femininity. Etiquette rules. Couture signifies. Regimen decrees Chopin piano, classical reading (Goethe and Schiller notably), church attendance, needlework, neighbourhood and *Kaffe und Kuchen* outings, and Miriam's own learning of German even as she seeks to impart 'good' English to those in her charge. Richardson keeps her lens highly particular, as though recording the instant-by-instant diary of Miriam's self-formation.

The novel, in a prime sense, bears upon Miriam's emergence yet also the feeling of being 'hemmed in' despite the apparent sisterhood of the French instructor Mademoiselle, the international phalanx of girls, and Fräulein Pfaff herself. She vacillates, given to 'English self-consciousness'. On a visit to Kreipe's restaurant in the village the novel says of her reaction to female passers-by, 'She had never seen women with so much decision in their bearing' (89). She recognises she could never meet the prerequisites of 'a happy German woman' (151). Her queries accumulate, whether negotiation of English and

German cultural difference, the impact of Darwin for her amid the churchgoing and the preachments of the Swiss Herr Pastor Lahmann and the Anglican Mr Brough, and doubts of efficacy as a teacher while remembering her English girlhood schooling. 'This is no place for *me*' (151) she vows finally, her last sight emblematically that of the railway station as she embarks on new tracks.

A voluminous reader herself, Shakespeare to Browning, and of histories like those of John Lothrop Motley, Richardson has Miriam recall being asked by her one-time vice-principal in England what she and fellow pupils would like best in life. Her answer has been 'to write a book' (80). The life 'her' book will tell, and the modern focus and means of its telling, is precisely that created in turn by Dorothy Richardson and which will extend into the ensuing entry-pages of the whole Pilgrimage series.

Jean Rhys, almost by rote, wins regard for *Wide Sargasso Sea*, her novel at once postcolonial and intertextual landmark. Her woman-alone fictions, *Quartet* (1928), *After Leaving Mr. Mackenzie* (1931), *Voyage in the Dark* (1924) and *Good Morning, Midnight* (1939), long have retreated beneath its shadow.[5] Story-collections to include *Tigers Are Better Looking* (1968), or the self-chronicle of *Smile Please: An Unfinished Autobiography* (post. 1979), similarly have existed more than not at the periphery of attention. Readerships coming to *Wide Sargasso Sea* from *Jane Eyre*, moreover, initially gave it recognition on the basis of the earlier novel. Charlotte Brontë's Bertha Rochester, unlike Rhys's Antoinette Cosway, is little more than gothic haunt or shadow. *Jane Eyre* has her positioned as follows:

> She was kept in very close confinement . . . people even for some years were not absolutely certain of her existence. No one saw her: . . . and who or what she was it is difficult to conjecture. They said Mr Edward had brought her back from abroad, and some believed she had been his mistress . . . This lady, ma'am, . . . turned out to be Mr Rochester's wife![6]

Madwoman in the Attic takes over, the enduring gloss.

It does no disservice to think the narrational aplomb of *Wide Sargasso Sea* at the very least equals, even outreaches, that of *Jane Eyre*.[7] Nor is that the case simply on grounds that Rhys's novel, paradoxically, doubles as a species of prequel despite its far later publication. The plot line indeed pursues the transposition of Antoinette Cosway into Bertha Mason, and then into Bertha Rochester, in the post-slavery Caribbean 1830s with to follow Atlantic removal to England and the closing events at Thornfield Hall. But unlike the sequential autobiography of *Jane Eyre* it does in memorial episodes, 'modern' collage.

'"They tell me I am in England but I don't believe them".'[8] So witnesses the incarcerated Bertha to her English nurse-keeper Grace Poole in *Wide Sargasso Sea*. Well might Rhys have her fantasise in the wake of confinement and the dislocation from planter Jamaica and Dominica to landed-manor England. How, for the psychologically uncentred Bertha as she has become, to calibrate the tropical Caribbean of 'all the people in my life' (32) with her English seignorial husband and his unceremonious servant? Even language has been upended, island vernacular, French and Spanish, as against the properness of Empire English. Rhys's feat goes infinitely beyond ostensible prelude. In the alternate registers of Bertha and Rochester, their imperfect understandings, she not only re-stories where and why 'Bertha' has arisen but re-styles Charlotte Brontë's storying.

That begins from the opening kaleidoscope of the Coulibri Estate, actual enough in the wake of Emancipation, but now under the filtering imagination of Antoinette as virtually other-world. Startling Antillean hyper-green prevails. Growths of fern, root, orchid, have become 'wild', the circumstantial terrain 'dead flowers mixed with fresh living smell' (4). Lotus-like somnolence has taken over ('No more slavery – why should *anybody* work?', 5), and yet human ferocity erupts, the violent gnaw of discrepant power among white, black and Creole. Turmoil stirs and contrasts, the island lushness, the mother Annette's poisoned horse, Daniel Cosway's unhinged letter alleging the family madness, the analogous two estate fires, and black Jamaican resentment at residual white planter presence. Rhys depicts topography full of history, though as implied in the landless Sargasso sea of the novel's title, dislocated, off-tilt.

Bertha's rite of passage towards marriage with Edward Rochester falls under precisely this kind of vista. Her widowed Martinique mother will edge towards madness within the Mason family. Her retarded step-brother Pierre will die a fire-death at the hands of dispossessed Jamaicans. The tough-love protection by the obeah-woman Christophine situates her, the light Creole, within animist

African lore even as she aspires to full white Christian gentility at the convent school in Spanish Town. Rhys lays out the novel's emblematic guidelines subtly, without rigid or undue insistence.

A classic domestic painting of 'white' England, 'The Miller's Daughter', contrasts against French-speaking green parrot Coco and its feared voodoo meaning. Amélie, Bertha's black friend and counterpart who will sexually betray her with Rochester, asks 'Is it true ... that England is like a dream ... London ... a cold, dark dream sometimes?' (65). Chimera, illusion, consort with actuality at every turn in Bertha's life, the challenge of finding centre amid the un-centring deflections of her life. Rhys keeps her eye sharp, her style watchful.

Postcolonial readings of the novel have done duty. Slavery, sugar wealth, and the kind of intruder greed embodied in the Mason and Rochester families, reflect the larger imperial drama. That extends to possession of Bertha, marriageable property but in breakdown also spousal damaged goods. Skin, hue, sexual-racial mix fittingly produce a storm of word-hatred. 'White cockroach' recurs. During the Coulibri conflagration shouts of 'black Englishman, white niggers' (35) fill the air. If as Christophine says of Bertha, 'She is a Creole girl, and she have the sun in her' (130), then the comment Grace Poole makes on the letter of employment sent by Rochester equally applies: *'that girl who lives in her own darkness'* (146). Their testimonies capture but do not resolve the divide within Bertha, the more so when candle in hand she begins her liberating final arson from English captivity.

The patterns within *Wide Sargasso Sea* work always to well-taken purpose. Antoinette into Bertha embodies both pomp and fall. Richard Mason or Edward Rochester find their male-proprietary entitlement subverted, even mocked. Memory serves as split mirror for the Cosways, for Mason (father and son), for Rochester, and for the Christophine families. Household etiquette plays against island spontaneity, the one fire or marriage against the other, tea against rum. The dialectics of Rhys's narrative, supported by the qualities of her local picturing, render the novel at ease in its espousal of the authorial modern.

Imagist poem, biographical autofiction or Caribbean-Atlantic fable, each achieves new expressive investiture for the woman's story being

132   MODERNS – CHAUCER TO CONTEMPORARY FICTION

told. The gendering of the texts, women's as against men's, will likely persist in debate. Women's modern, as these writings are justly to be construed, belong on more agreed ground. For the modern in Loy, Richardson and Rhys, across genres, belongs in the overall body of writing now heralded as modernist. To speak in this regard only of an avant-garde does not quite go far enough. Theirs has longer reach, more extensive spectrum, to be recognised as belonging to the first and then the inter-generational passage of Long Modernism.

Notes

1. Virginia Woolf, *A Room of One's Own*, Harmondsworth, Middlesex: Penguin Books, 1967, 107.
2. Mina Loy, *Lunar Baedeker*, Paris: Contact Publishing, 1923, republished as *Lunar Baedeker and Time-Tables*, Highlands/Black Mountain, NC: Jargon Press, 1958; *Insel*, Los Angeles: Black Sparrow Press, 1991; *Stories and Essays*, Dalkey Archive Press, 2011. The key other collection is Roger L. Conover (ed.), *The Lost Lunar Baedeker: Poems of Mina Loy*, New York: The Noonday Press, 1999. *Feminist Manifesto* is to be found (an inaccurate version) in Robert L. Conover (ed.), *Last Lunar Baedeker*, 1982, then Noonday Press, 1999. Relevant studies include Isabel Castelao-Gómez, 'The Art of Life, the Dance of Poetry: Gender, Experiment and Experience in Mina Loy and Diane di Prima', *Miscélanea: A Journal of English and American Studies*, 56, 2017, 33–56; Carolyn Burke, *Becoming Modern: The Life of Mina Loy*, Berkeley: University of California Press, 1996; Maeera Schreiber and Keith Tuma (eds), *Mina Loy: Woman and Poet*, The National Poetry Foundation, 1980.
3. This and all subsequent references are to Conover, *The Lost Lunar Baedeker: Poems of Mina Loy*, 154.
4. English publication of the Pilgrimage novels are as follows: *Pointed Roofs*, London: Duckworth, 1915; *Backwater*, London: Duckworth, 1916; *Honeycomb*, London: Duckworth, 1917; *The Tunnel*, London: Duckworth, 1919; *Interim*, London: Duckworth, 1919; *Deadlock*, London: Duckworth, 1921; *Revolving Lights*, London: Duckworth, 1923; *The Trap*, London: Duckworth, 1925; *Oberland*, London: Duckworth, 1927; *Dawn's Left Hand*, London: Duckworth, 1931; and *Clear Horizon*, London: J. M. Dent & The Cresset Press, 1935. Collected editions are *Pilgrimage*, 4 vols, London: J. M. Dent & The Cresset Press, to include *Dimple Hill* for the first time, 1938; *Pilgrimage*, 4 vols, London: J. M. Dent, 1967, to include *March Moonlight* for the first time; and *Pilgrimage*, 4 vols, London: Virago, 1979. All page references are to this latter edition, Virago, 1979.

5. For a keenly attentive synopsis of Rhys's other fiction, see James Wood, 'The Many Confrontations of Jean Rhys', *The New Yorker*, 11 and 18 July 2022.
6. Charlotte Brontë, *Jane Eyre*, 1847, Harmondsworth, Middlesex: Penguin Books, 1953, 421.
7. The standard account has to be Sandra M. Gilbert and Susan Gubar, *The Madwoman in the Attic: The Woman Writer and the Nineteenth-Century Literary Imagination*, New Haven, CT: Yale University Press, 1969. A range of other bearings apply, notably: Marta Caminero-Santangelo, *The Madwoman Can't Speak: Or Why Insanity is Not Subversive*, Ithaca, NY: Cornell University Press, 1998; Elsie B. Michie, *Outside the Pale: Cultural Exclusion, Gender Difference and the Victorian Woman Writer*, Ithaca, NY: Cornell University Press, 1993; Germaine Greer, *The Madwoman's Underclothes: Essays and Occasional Writings*, London: Picador, 1986; Elaine Showalter, *A Literature of Their Own: British Women Novelists from Brontë to Lessing*, Princeton, NJ: Princeton University Press, 1977; and Ellen Moers, *Literary Women: The Great Writers*, New York: Oxford University Press, 1977.
8. Jean Rhys, *Wide Sargasso Sea*, Harmondsworth, Middlesex: Penguin Books, 1968, 2001, 117. All page references are to this edition. I have much benefited from Miranda Seymour, *I Used to Live Here Once: The Haunted Life of Jean Rhys*, New York: Norton & Company, 2022.

CHAPTER 11

Postmodern Modern:
B. S. Johnson, Ann Quin

Harold Pinter's Nobel Prize address in 2005 may not provide the complete fit for the novels of B. S. Johnson or Ann Quin but it points in the right general direction:

> So language in art remains a highly ambiguous transaction, a quicksand, a trampoline, a frozen pool which might give way under you, the author, at any time.(2005)[1]

Narrative swing of pendulum, risk of language, assuredly made for unique style in the fictions of both writers. *The Unfortunates* (1969), Johnson's notorious novel in a box, immediately put him in a new league. *Berg* (1964), laconic *nouveau roman* with tinctures of both menace and the comic, likewise aligned Quin. To the extent that these novels, as their other fiction, won more than coterie notice in emerging from the 1960s they were taken not only to have arrived at, but stepped across, the doorstep of the postmodern.

Nor were Johnson and Quin flying solo. Joyce, Beckett or Robbe-Grillet may have provided inspirational sight lines but within English fiction a new 'new' was circling. Reynar Heppenstall's *The Connecting Door* (1962), first-person voyages to Germany set in the 1940s, uses memory-fracture and time-shift as befitted an author also drawn to *le nouveau roman*. Alan Burns's *Europe After The Rain* (1963), with its Max Ernst title and epistolary postcard format, delivers the neo-surreal vision of a devastated continent. Christine Brooke-Rose in *Such* (1966) transposes a psychiatry setting into the world seen as though on return from death. Bridgid Brophy puts the multiples of sexual identity under apposite wordplay and through the *mise-en-scène* of an airport lounge in *In Transit: An Heroi-Cyclic Novel* (1969). Eva Figes's *Light* (1983), her day-in-the-life of an ageing Monet, refracts the great

134

impressionist in a portrait itself provocatively impressionist. Other names, likewise duly innovative, accompany, notably John Fowles, J. G. Ballard and Angela Carter.[2]

The impatience of Johnson and Quin with existing standard-bearers became more than rumour. The working-class grit ushered in by the novels of Alan Sillitoe, John Wain or John Braine looked embattled, limited by earnestness. Kingsley Amis, and the line into Bradbury–Lodge domestic or campus satire, could entertain though not shake rafters. Stalwarts like William Golding or Iris Murdoch mattered albeit less for experimental colours. The generation of Martin Amis, its vehement articulacy, had still to win the prizes. Even the preceding modernist axis, Joyce or Eliot, had begun to look sufficiently honoured, due respect duly served.

Johnson, and Quin, insistently to their own flag and whatever the hubris, believed the English novel had fallen into timidity, un-ambition. Their pairing to an extent has been fortuitous, the happenstance of literary appetite for fresh departure. On the other hand it has about it a necessary rightness, namely, and however differingly, the ways in which their fiction goes beyond the modern into the postmodern.

Johnson's seven novels in all, together with the screen and radio productions, plays, poems, anthologies, reviews and reportage, add up to a flourish irredeemably cut short by his suicide in 1973. The energy was prodigious, the ambition formidable. Maybe a degree of bipolarity lay in the flux, the exuberance of creative risk-taking, the fear of defeat. Either way he gave notice of being always on front-line duty. The evidence lay plentifully to hand.

The fiction launches with *Travelling People* (1967), plurally voiced, a Round Britain travelogue of class demarcation and love soured, and continues through to *See The Old Lady Decently* published posthumously in 1975, a hallucinatory narrative of motherhood and his own conception and birth. An outlet for his keenly autobiographical poetry was to be found in *Penguin Modern Poets 25* (1975). His stage play, *You're Human Like the Rest of Them* (1964), anticipates the themes of friendship and illness taken up in *The Unfortunates*. The documentary he created for ITV, *Fat Man on a Beach* (1975), has Johnson going against usual expectation of format and to be seen uninterruptedly reading his work amid summer holidaymakers.

136   MODERNS – CHAUCER TO CONTEMPORARY FICTION

Rarely did he better indicate his direction of travel, its postmodern impulse, than in the ribbingly titled *Aren't You Rather Young to be Writing Your Memoirs?* (1973). He insists that the next stage of the literary modern should be to travel through Joyce as *magister ludi*, and then travel on, and into, ever newer reflexive loops. Other influences, Sterne in *Tristram Shandy*, or Beckett, whose *The Unnamable* supplies a prefatory quotation on the writer's situation for *Albert Angelo* (1964), won his loyalty for the same reason, art's artifice not just recognised but celebrated and built into the storytelling.

To seize upon *The Unfortunates* as entry-point is to be faced head-on with Johnson's symptomatic challenge. Novel-in-a-box, twenty-seven separate and mini-numbered brief chapters read at the reader's order of choosing, was this gimmick, mere deck of cards? Or was it genuine boldness of strike, Johnson's winning landmark? Estimation has not ceased to vacillate, though the heckles and out-of-print intervals lessen and the hurrahs have grown louder.[3]

No matter that precedents, known or not to Johnson, do in fact exist, whether Marc Saporta's stream of consciousness *La Quête* (*The Quest*, 1961) or Julio Cortázar's self-nominated anti-novel *Rayuela* (*Hopscotch*, 1963). Allowing for passing twists of page layout, nor had Johnson written Burroughs-like cut-up, his sentences for the most part in standard syntax. Postmodern, even so, seemed on point, the novel literally unbound from fixed book form and possessed of 'modern' narrative agency quite its own.

The sports journalist-narrator's soccer report pasted into the back inside box-cover, City v. United, gives hints of the text at hand (Johnson drew on having been sent by the *Observer* to cover a Notts versus Spurs match in Nottingham). 'SUB INSPIRES CITY TRIUMPH' reads the heading. 'From B. S. Johnson' posts the byline. The live-action style detailing runs of play, players, individual shots, offsides, tackles, free kicks, and a chance goal, does day-after Sunday newspaper duty. Tacitly it also hints at the author's messaging of his novel's performance, two fields, sport and text.

The guise of the remembering former sports-writer, Johnson himself or persona, allows for a similar double direction of memory. On the one hand he 'reports' the fond if combative friendship, and then ravage by cancer, of his literary-academic companion Tony (his actual last name of Tillinghast not given). On the other this folds into the more inward curve of Johnson's writer-life and ambition. The recurring mention of Tony's thesis on Boswell works to both purposes. In common with Samuel Johnson's amanuensis, Johnson clearly sees himself writing twin tracks, biography also autobiography.

Paired chapters, explicitly titled 'FIRST' and 'LAST', give framing, the former addressed to finding the 'order' amid 'disintegration' personified in Tony, the latter under one of Johnson's several fighting maxims: 'In general generalization is to lie, to tell lies'. Points of entry into the story-infolds, their lengths differing, evidently remain optional. Johnson's offer of reader choice could easily have slipped towards confusion, mere randomness. In the event Johnson has *The Unfortunates* cohere, the better sum of parts.

'That was the first time', as the section is labelled, remembers shared interest in university student-magazine editing, Johnson at King's College London, Tony at the always un-named Nottingham University. The aftermath will be intellectual liaison, visits, correspondence, talk, notably about Johnson's first novels *Travelling People* (1963) and *Albert Angelo* (1964), and Tony's ongoing Augustan-period literary scholarship. 'The four of us together' summons overlaps of marriage, Johnson and Ginny, Tony and June, their forms of coupledom, pub outings, and the occasional spats. The refractions knit, bonds of friendship and the writing life.

'At least once he visited us at the Angel' acts as a contrarium of remembrance with Tony using the British Museum Library, his saliva failing from medical treatment, and a visit to see *Play* by Beckett. 'That short occasion in Brighton', with Tony's lectures to overseas students, marks his beginning illness, tiredness the first pointer towards tumours and cancer. 'For recuperation, after the first treatment' again veers several ways at once, the setting the solid Brighton of Tony's parents, Johnson fretting at his lost romance with Wendy, bookshops, and Tony ill if 'outwardly' looking in health. 'June rang on Saturday' reads as abrupt in word as in the news of Tony's death that it conveys. Death-in-life becomes meditation, Johnson's purview of transience and the writer.

At the same time he sees his authorship, newspaper or novel, located in specific time and place ('it's almost two . . . I must get to the ground'). As reporter he observes 'The pitch worn, the worn patrons', and beyond the stadium, the architecture of the city and its station, the streets, buses and shop fronts. As novelist he has misgivings about journalism ('Let's get on with the bloody job'). His thoughts turn to heavier-duty creative writing. 'I had a lovely

138   MODERNS – CHAUCER TO CONTEMPORARY FICTION

flat then', he remembers at one point, invoking himself the writer at his desk, the commitment but also the frustration. 'I was not big enough to write it', he says of the novel that will become *House Mother Normal*.

In 'The opera singer the Easter before Finals' he looks back to a 'failed affair' at the same time that he is arguing with Tony about the role of literary criticism. Whether Johnson or Tony has the right of it, their exchanges again affirm Johnson's belief in the seriousness of his call:

> To Tony, the criticism of literature was a study, a pursuit, a discipline of the highest kind in itself; to me, I told him, the only use of criticism was if it helped people write better books . . . That period was a fertile one, it seemed the closer Finals came, the more I wanted to write myself.

The author to his calling lies at the heart of *The Unfortunates*.

Appetite becomes accompanying metaphor. Allusions to his overweight and drinking (in a Sterneian gesture he ends one section with 'But first the gents') alternate with his need to feed the page. The chapters, in whichever sequence they are read, leave no doubt of fullness of thread and segue, the single but decidedly ample narrative track. To this end they can be said to have been energetically subbed, as it were, by Johnson himself as his novel's postmodern team manager.

House Mother Normal sees publication just past midway in Johnson's novel-writing career, seven geriatric 'talking' heads at dinner table in their care home followed by the authorial report card of their sexually off-centre younger guardian 'House Mother'. Each interior monologue vacillates between splinters of past memory, and envies and sometimes angers, towards present-day fellow residents. Personal histories accumulate of marriages, work, wartime, pubs, drift, aloneness. Time-now comprises fatuous games like Pass the Parcel, the singing of the false-hearty '*The joys of life continue strong/ Throughout old age*', the gluing of crêpe decorations, messy eating and spillage, mops, spit bowls, and always body-for-body medical ailment.[4]

Johnson's part, grimly but far from unsympathetically, is to devise wording, and so to speak un-wording, of life at death's edge, the last exit. The repeated end-tag of 'No, doesn't matter' hints of finality to come. His galleried speakers he projects as animate left-overs, marooned cells with NERs (explained as No Effective Relatives). Told in separate twenty-one-page sections, the descending order of the mental decline of the residents Johnson reflects in the page's selective word snippets and discrepant typography.

Starting from Sarah Lamson's 'I tell them my troubles, they tell me theirs' (19) as more or less remembered family and marital history the monologues extend to the staccato half-words and left-in-blank pages of George Hedbury ('spitting spitting spitting', 8) and Rosetta Stanton ('I am a prisoner of myself', 15). Rosetta's open-space pages also echo language as frequently Welsh as English, herself lost in both. The voices between likewise variously summon event, remonstrate, or barely make it into utterance.[5]

Charlie Edwards, gassed war veteran, one-time cinema pianist, street penny-whistler, lover of lamb chops, imagines himself the sexual suitor of the crumbling Mrs Ridge. Ivy Nicholls, self-distant, wanders in mind back to the lost routine of suburban living, the Women's Institute and Southend bungalows. Ron Lamson, venomously in pain with haemorrhoids, his hands sticky with the Social Evening glue, gives way to the mental unglue of 'My memory's playing me up again' (16). The phrase could be said to give a motto to the novel overall. Gloria Ridge, more coherent than most, harbours the image of 'my one true love' (11) before having given herself to serial promiscuity. Sioned Bowen, thinking back to her unwanted life as a servant in the local country Great Hall, veers into the memory of upper-class malfeasance. Johnson aligns the portraiture interactively, a novel of mutual refractions.

The medical charts that precede the monologues encrypt dark prophecy of degree zero. The CQ or Cultural Intelligence Count measures receding mind. Age afflictions range from osteo-arthritis to senility. The assignment of final word, and action, to the House Mother does key narrative duty. She delivers the last panorama ('This is my Empire', 8), the show of authoritarian hand ('Treat them like children', 3), and the remembrance of other geriatric regimes ('where confused patients ate each other's puke', 15). Life moving into death becomes her theme, the residents successively named for their pluses and minuses. In the final sex scene with Ralphie the dog, herself naked, vaginal, her strip-show in front of those under care becomes 'sport' as she calls it, grotesque ironic climax in the face of nadir.

Johnson, however, is not wholly done. An epilogue is granted. He has her 'step outside convention', the only speaker given twenty-two pages:

> Thus you see I too am the puppet or concoction of a writer (you always knew there was a writer behind it all? Ah, there's no fooling you readers!), a writer who has me at present standing in the post-orgasmic nude but who still expects me to be his words without embarrassment or personal comfort. So you see this is from his skull! (22)

Johnson's literary signal holds for *House Mother Normal* but also at large for his fiction. Author authors character. Character authors author. Reader ('you see') is brought into collusion. The postmodern modern has engaged, B. S. Johnson one of its inescapable English avatars.

Ann Quin's *Berg* served notice at the outset that her reader had decisions to make. That the story of Alistair Charles Humphrey Berg opens with one of modern fiction's most memorable lines immediately puts the cat among the pigeons: 'A man called Berg, who changed his name to Greb, came to a seaside town intending to kill his father'.[6] Berg/Greb is in himself the first of the novel's disarrangements. Screens, listenings-in, the voyeuristic, flashbacks of memory and voice, letters, a mother's verbal and incestuous cosseting of her son, a ventriloquist's dummy for supposed corpse, newspaper headlines, even a comic police station scene, disrupt any actual parricide. A Brighton world bordering on Grand Guignol holds sway.

Was this first novel in any way to be understood some new wave crime story? How to un-code the ironic deadpan of style, third and first person, the dark hallucinatory inflections and fades? If this was fiction in postmodern mode it brought challenge, no unearned reader interpretation. Over time, as with *Three* (1966), *Passages* (1969) and *Tripticks* (1972), consensus has begun to form. Quin matters, her authorship an important forward edge. Attributing maverick status simply avoids the kind of breakthrough she had reason to believe she was attempting.

A gothic trio assembles, Berg the hair treatment salesman and frustrated musician, Nathaniel the feckless drink-addled father who has played the music halls, and Judith Goldstein, ripe, ready-for-action lover and floozy. They could readily be seen and heard as inhabiting Pinter or Joe Orton theatre. The fourth presence finds both voice-off and embodiment in Berg's mother Edith, son-fixated, his assiduous pursuer from possessive over-fuss in childhood to back and forth love-letters. Ali, as she calls him, does stand-in for Nathy (Nathaniel), the absconded husband. Berg, above all, lives as much in and as fantasy as fact, his mind haunted, his life a string of un-ravellings. Serio-farce, *Berg* so positions the would-be hitman as small-time Hamlet, Oedipal son never to complete his task, unlike Graham Greene's other Brighton pathological misfit Pinkie.

Quin's use of seedy, out-of-season guesthouse as location creates *huis clos*, the novel's pressure-chamber of being. Cracked ceiling, gas ring, plastic tablecloth, strewn clothing, sparse wardrobe, a screen for repair works between rooms, all point to degree zero for Berg. Strewn clothes, extravagant dressing gown, pets, copious lipstick, make-up and shampoos make for Judith. Across the road the Palais de Dance jangles with near-phantom music and voices. Sea alternates between calm and chill, streets run bare, windowpanes cloud with frost. Landlady and the nag of overdue rent feature. Seaside ice cream alternates with eggs and bacon fry-ups. Beckett tramps hover outside, sympathetic choruses and threat-figures. The railway station becomes the illusory No Exit, open and yet closed door.

Throughout *Berg* these insistently prosaic features intersect with the novel's psychodrama, the interior black comedy buttressed with footfalls of Sophocles, Shakespeare and Freud. Plot parodies itself. Berg, sleuth at least by intent, is termed 'a Pirandello hero'(54), the faux revenger in search of self-authoring. This is the Berg with 'mixed murmurings in his head' (82) who will try to become his father and, thereby, become the lover both of Judith and his mother. One of Berg's pamphlets reads 'BUY BERG'S BEST TONIC DEFEAT DELILAH'S DAMAGE: IN TWO MONTHS YOU WILL BE A NEW MAN' (11). The implications tease exquisitely, the Bible's Samson, severed hair, and 'you will be a new man'.

Berg's alienation is both highlighted and mocked. He will sling Judith's cat at a wall as though to perform a surrogate killing. He will think he has killed her caged budgie. In a scene of sublime grotesquerie he will cross-dress as Judith only to become the object of sexual aggression by the drunken Nathaniel. The black comedy turns blacker. In a denouement of sorts in which he feels 'almost

142   MODERNS – CHAUCER TO CONTEMPORARY FICTION

Lilliputian' (137), he mutilates his father's dummy under the illusion that he is truly avenging Edith for her spouse's abandonment of herself and son. 'I have to report my father's missing' (155) he tells the police, comic local Oedipus, fantasy murderer. Quin has her sights on the sensation of self held against itself, caught under self-arrest. The fault lines taken up in *Berg* see the modern condition becoming postmodern, the one written into and at the same time over the other.

Three continues the thrust of its predecessor, its title a pointer to Quin's ensuing subversion of binaries, be they coupledom, sexuality, love–hate, even schizophrenia. Triangulation, as in *Berg*, serves as index, starting with the infinitely middle-class couple, Leonard (L) and Ruth (R), and their young woman lodger (S). The single-letter initials open into three-voice mosaic, overlapping ledgers of self-loss, nested desire. L displaces love into cultivation of orchids. R over-lavishes affection on her cat Bobo. S keeps obsessive minute journals. Sexual contact veers from R's avoidance to R and L's shared bathtub fantasy to L's act of rape. Quin writes as witness for the prosecution against coupled lives lost in banality, claustrophobic envy of the dead S.

Quin said often that she thought *L'Année Dernière à Marienbad*, the 1961 Robbe-Grillet/Resnais *ciné-novel*, the exemplary modern composition, above all its threefold intersections of memory. Her novel's ménage-à-trois of L, the closed-off working translator, his wife the hausfrau under neurasthenic headache and stress, and S, projected figure of enviable transgression driven to likely water suicide, resides not only in the actuality of their co-habitation. It lies in the highly detailed and indeterminate reflections of consciousness they exert upon each other.

Footfalls press from the trinary logic of Aristotle to the Christian trinity. Local specifics span L's holocaust war memory of three gallows, R's bouts of unfeeling ('Three months of living with two people and not any nearer – nearer', 92), a hotel three beds, and L's being beaten up by three men. The markers at the same time are those of stasis: 'In silence they ate' (65); 'Cigarette smoke formed a screen between them' (67); 'Confronted by an existence I can no longer believe in' (137); 'I see him as from a cage' (141). Their speech one to the other becomes barbed marital infantilism ('What's for din-dins?', 60). The lifelessness of the garden statues in the father-in-law's Grey House makes for appropriate commentary.

Only S personifies ventilation, the appetite implied in her vertically laid out listings of sights, adventures, animals, nature, mobility, Dickens and other reading. Yet however these contrast with the deadening norms about her, they do not prevent her drowning or the guilt L and R hide on account of their deviation from the life-example she embodies. *Three* records this vision of life-death in string-sequences of internal narrative, journal entries, played-over tape recordings, remembered dinner table and bedtime etiquette, and the three of them acting out white-robed mime dramas. Quin's postmodern forte throughout the novel attaches to sublimation and its workings, scenarios of surface depth.

In *Passages* and *Tripticks* Quin ventures further into hyper-reality. Both operate, insistently, against 'realist' criterion, the former, with its chimera setting of Greece under the colonels and the quest of a lover-pair for a lost brother, and the latter, with its text-and-image satiric facsimile of billboard America and Kerouac's *On the Road* macho bromance. *The Unmapped Country: Stories & Fragments* (post. 2018), autofictions, stories, even her self-parody as experimentalist, throws explanatory light on Quin's resolve to give the modern in her fiction its postmodern charge.

Like all generic nomenclature, postmodern needs pliancy in application. Whether in literature, or across the other arts, it steers for a negotiation between generality and the particular. Neither Johnson nor Quin unduly relished the label but interpretation has found it advantageous to construe writing whose reflexive formatting is a given. Both authors made clear they thought modernism per se had done duty if not run its course. What, then, next? *The Unfortunates* and *Berg*, and the accompanying novels by their authors, signify another evolution, in each venture and insistently on their own narrative terms that of the postmodern modern.

Notes

1. Harold Pinter, Nobel Prize address, 2005.
2. Rayner Heppenstall, *The Connecting Door*, London: Barrie & Rockiff, 1962: Alan Burns, *Europe After the Rain*, London: Calder, 1965; Christine Brooke-Rose, *Such*, London: Michael Joseph, 1966; Brigid Brophy, *In Transit: An Heroi-Cyclic Novel*, London: MacDonald, 1969; Eva Figes, *Light*, London: Hamish Hamilton, 1983.

144 MODERNS – CHAUCER TO CONTEMPORARY FICTION

3. The definitive critical biography remains Jonathan Coe, *Like a Fiery Elephant: The Story of B. S. Johnson*, London: Picador, 2004. Bibliography for the novels runs as follows: *Travelling People*, London: Constable, 1963; *Albert Angelo*, London: Constable, 1964; *Trawl*, London: Secker & Warburg, 1966; *The Unfortunates*, London: Panther Books in association with Secker & Warburg, 1969; *House Mother Normal: A Geriatric Comedy*, London: Collins, 1971; *Christie Malry's Own Double-Entry*, London: Collins, 1973: *See the Old Lady Decently*, London: Hutchinson, 1975.

4. Page references are to *B. S. Johnson Omnibus: Albert Angelo, Trawl, House Mother Normal*, London: Macmillan, Picador, 2004.

5. Coe points out that Johnson found an important influence as to format in Philip Toynbee's novel *Tea with Mrs Goodman*, London: Horizon, 1947. It would be hard to resist some comparison for setting with Ken Kesey, *One Flew Over the Cuckoo's Nest*, New York: Viking Press, 1962, and Kingsley Amis, *Ending Up*, London: Cape, 1973.

6. Quin has been notoriously unavailable until recently and in limited re-issues by the Dalkey Archive Press. For ease of convenience, page references are to the ebook edition. *Berg*, 9.

CHAPTER 12

Contemporary Modern: Six Fictions

The novels that lead *Moderns* towards a provisional close indicate a shift not necessarily of tectonic plate but of compass. Caribbean and African, Asian, Jewish, Gay: these, in kind with other auspices of 'English' story, not only add to the widening but the interiorisation of perspective. That is not to suggest some want of antecedent or coeval writing. Barbadian and British co-exist in the authorship of George Lamming as does Trinidad in Monique Roffey, Jamaica in Zadie Smith. Names like Buchi Emecheta or Ben Okri write Africa, in their case Nigeria, into British fiction. Asian Britain has its voice in novels to span Salman Rushdie, Hanif Kureishi or Monica Ali. Jewish Britain, whether Clive Sinclair, Bernice Rubens or Elaine Feinstein, takes up and transforms a tradition going back to Disraeli. Same-sex gendering holds for the writing of Paul Bailey, Sarah Waters or Jeanette Winterson.[1] Plurality of voice not only plays across these contemporary moderns, but that of the writers within each legacy, be it ethnic or sexual.

Nor does it sidestep the flourish of established other contemporaries, whether Martin Amis, Anita Brookner, Julian Barnes, Ian McEwan, A. S. Byatt or Angela Carter, or prodigious extra-British authors like Kazuo Ishiguro and Abdulrazak Gurnah. But the six novels at hand, in new optics, and in new reaches of voice, give latest albeit even so still selective embodiment to the contemporary modern sight line of English fiction.

Bernardine Evaristo's *Girl, Woman, Other* (2019), in orchestrating Afro-womanism across London, Nigeria and California, opts for gynocentric multiples and polyphony. Kamila Shamsie's *Home Fire* (2017), as dynastic political novel of Pakistani Britain with framing from Sophocles's *Antigone*, confronts assimilation and its discontents. Open Diran Adebayo's *Some Kind of Black* (1996) and enter 1990s diversely black London, its storyline a cat's-cradle of self-identity within the novel's city of allegiances.

145

Xiaolu Guo's *A Concise Chinese–English Dictionary for Lovers* (2007) gives deliberate broken-English but poetic diary to the Passage to England of Zhuang Xiao Qiao, her life in China, London and Europe at once juncture and discordance not only of languages but perception of the world.[2] Howard Jacobson's *The Finkler Question* (2010) holds the mirror to modern Jewishness, being Jewish, acting on being Jewish, seeking to be Jewish, a novel full of wry-sardonic contemplation as to ancestral yet contemporary heritage. For Alan Hollinghurst in *The Line of Beauty* (2004), the refractions of gay sexuality, cocaine, Oxford, Thatcher-era Toryism and Kensington London unfold with meticulous eloquence.[3]

No work of fiction ever truly assumes symptomatic status. Literary work, rather, across genre and spectrum, invariably contributes to creation of the very era in which it makes its bow. 'But how could you live and have no story to tell?', asks Fyodor Dostoevsky, in his 'White Nights' (1848).[4] 'I like the human imagination, its brutal, aggressive energy, its profundity, its power to transform the material world into art', asserts Hanif Kureishi in *Intimacy* (1998).[5] Both observations suggest pointers to the several novels under review. Given differing directions and strengths, they are advanced as doing precisely that, at once imaginatively self-standing and indicative of momentum in the making of the new literary modern.

Girl, Woman, Other has about it a kind of deceptive matter-of-factness. Bernardine Evaristo's insider panels of black women's lives each are told from the ground up, yet linked into larger mosaics of identity, power and not the least geography. South London in point of departure, the novel branches from borough to borough to Opolo in the Niger Delta, the American Eastern Seaboard, West Hollywood and coastal Barbados, along with England's Leeds, Plymouth and Hebden Bridge. Beginning from Amma Bonsu, gay radical feminist and author of the play *The Last Amazon of Dahomey*, and returning to the larger ensemble of the last chapter ('The After-Party'), the women embody different orders of Afro-Englishness, a chain of kinship for the girl, woman, other of Evaristo's title. The map reads bracingly, the contemporary modern of England under female gendered black lens.

Lives comes over busy in detail, school friends grown into adulthood, co-workers, lovers, activists. The Dedication offers vernacular enumeration, 'sisters', 'sistas' and 'sistahs', and 'wimmin' and 'the

CONTEMPORARY MODERN   147

womyn'. Amma takes point position, early to come out sexually, Deptford squatter (the community named Freedomia), mother to the transgender Yazz ('Yazz was going to be her countercultural experiment', 36). Dominique, her friend, becomes the actress who will eventually move to Hollywood after her intense love–hate relationship with the pathologically exclusionist African American Nzinga. The contrasts, and the brackets, accumulate.

Carole, academic high-flyer in mathematics, will enter the City as high paid and high coutured heels and lipstick economist. La Tisha, rebel at school, becomes supermarket supervisor and 'Chief Fucking Bitch on the prowl' (189). Shirley, history graduate, seeks to be upbeat mentor to her state school school-kids despite the mediocrity of her marriage. Megan, woke to a fault, non-binary, and after steering through hostile parents, transgenders to Morgan, and moves from the London south to the rural north with the also transgender Bibi into an ecological life of self-sufficiency – paired black faces in the English countryside. Hattie, matriarch at eighty-three, provides un-patriarchal standing, Grace the wife-witness to poor sex-in-marriage and childbearing. These, serendipitously, steer into and out of each other's histories, different but interconnecting Englishwomen of colour.

Evaristo has class enter at every turn. Tough estate housing exists alongside Thameside black theatre, cleaner and supermarket employment alongside high finance in the City. Grandmother kitchen and 'baby mother' pram signify stages in the history of black English womanhood. Teacher and campus English gets spoken alongside street girl argot or dub. Each woman embodies her story for itself yet also for its connecting tissue: mother and daughter, win and loss, and sexualities straight, gay, bi, trans, fertile and menopausal. Nor do other contexts go missing. Interracial condescension arises in the figure of the white South African figure of Penelope and her employment of Bummi, Carole's Nigerian mother, as cleaner. Frequent in-house black misogyny gets its recognition. The novel makes no concessions to pc black or white.

Evaristo eschews capital letters for her sentences and paragraphs as if to give the novel oral as much as scriptural storytelling fluency. Few would doubt that it pays dividends. An implicit overview for *Girl, Woman, Other* issues from Shirley King. The outset of her career in the classroom in a working-class comprehensive school begins in hope:

> Shirley felt the pressure was now on to be a great teacher and an ambassador for every black person in the world. (222)

The high ambition assuredly belongs to an invented character, and for the personage involved whose times will meet downs as often as successes. But there can be justified grounds for thinking it attaches in scale to Evaristo's literary ambassadorship, her 'English' black embassy of women accorded appropriate contemporary aliveness of idiom.

Wembley. ISIS. Preston Road. Raqqa. The coordinates for Kamila Shamsie's *Home Fire* reach deep into different conjugations of England home and away. In the British-born but Pakistan-legacied twins Aneeka and Parvaiz and their lawyer elder sister Isma, and England's Home Secretary Karamat Lone and his son Eamonn, the novel keeps its family threads busy, boldly laced. Geographies embrace the North Circular and Karachi, with Amherst and Istanbul in the mapping. Language resources run from London argot and airport security interrogation to Urdu and Arabic both vernacular and Koranic. Tactically, and without acceding to formula, it shades the Antigone story of mirror-fatherhoods, sibling assassination, and en-coffining into Anglo-Asian auspices. Shamsie works these fronts with touch, her narrative of the generational modern of Pakistani England.

The storytelling moves into, and through, engaging ambiguities. The one father, Adil Pasha, his daughter Isma describes as 'guitarist, gambler, con man, jihadi – but he was most consistent in the role of absentee father' (47). Speculation persists as to whether he has been killed at Raqqa as ISIS insurgent or en route to and even in Guantanamo. Either way he will spook his family, and most of all his son Parvaiz, youthful electronics-whizz and sound designer, as he heeds, and then attempts to step back from, the bloodier manifestations of the call to become a warrior for Caliphate under the recruitment of the false mentor Farooq in London.

The other father, Karamat Lone, Bradford business millionaire and Tory top politico, has embraced Union Jack Britishness with a vengeance though never without wariness. One of his speeches runs, 'There is nothing this country won't allow you to achieve – Olympic medals, captaincy of the cricket team, pop stardom, reality TV crowns. And if none of that works out, you can settle for being Home Secretary' (89). Not unwillingly he carries the burdens of being an Asian 'first', ready to play tough on migration and to cede Islam to public church-going. His son, in turn, will relax insouciantly on his father's money and political caché, the gentrified lounger who becomes Aneeka's lover.

Shamsie's 'ethnic' England comes over as multi-highway. Secularism and mosque vie. Suburban normalcy (nicely pointed references to *The Great British Bake Off* recur) vies with Muslims or post-Muslims who find themselves accused, shadowed at least, by images of jihad and the attention of an MI5 in charge of counter-terror. Purpose and cross-purpose overlap, whether Aneeka's affair with Eamonn as ruse to help her brother extricate himself from the jihadi network or Pavaiz's botched action in thinking he can parlay his way via the British embassy back to England. Can he be repatriated, the Pakistani Brit or British Pakistani? The final spectacle of brother-sister and lover death, Sophocles updated and now televised internationally, throws dramatic light upon a west and Middle East caught the several ways at once. The novel, to its imaginative credit, keeps the chilling denouement not only credible but proportionate.

Westminster and Karachi, UK parliament and Islamic martyrdom, politics and media: *Home Fire* avails itself of immediacy, irrefragable modern fare. Yet in having the novel say of Pavaiz that 'he didn't know how to break free of these currents of history' (171) Shamsie locates the storyline not only in England but in the altogether larger spread of UK/Pakistan hybridity, contemporary modern history, contemporary modern telling.

'Sorry of my English' (2). Xiaolu Guo's *A Concise Chinese–English Dictionary for Lovers* tells a Passage to England both pilgrim's progress and love story. The apology for broken English does necessary opening business, Zuang Xiao Quiao/Z's crossing from the one language to the other and from Beijing Airport to Heathrow the beginning of the process whereby she herself becomes the embodied dictionary of the two cultures. The space and time of ancestral China and the congestion of metro-modern London contend ('The day I arrived to the West, I suddenly realized I was Chinese', 186). The novel's culture-filtering, Chinese collectivism as against western individuality, state as against private art, usages like 'revolutionary' or 'be my guest', become life and book 'entries' to ingenious good purpose.

'Soon I stealing their language too' (18) attests the twenty-three-year-old Z, newly enrolled in language school and having snaffled café utensils and edibles for her meagre Nuttington House lodging near Baker Street. Other signposting gathers. Her Chinese passport has been 'bending in my pocket' (3). Heathrow has confronted her with the categories ALIEN and NON ALIEN. Her 'Concise' dictionary serves as 'the "most important thing from China"' (10). Full English breakfast contrasts with Full Chinese breakfast. The Tube map reads 'like plate of noodles' (19). Rudeness in *Chop Chop*, a Cantonese-Chinese restaurant, causes her to say 'I am shameful for being Chinese' (75). She wonders if she has metamorphosed into a kind of Red Guard living in England and at the same time orientalist stereotype ('I am barbarian, illiterate peasant girl, a face of third world, and irresponsible foreigner', 154). These Z puts through her contrasts of language, whether four-tone Chinese intonation or the nuances of English grammar's 'should' as conditional, and whether Mao's *Little Red Book* or Virginia Woolf's *To The Lighthouse* ('I am in a hurry to understand all these words', 190) best suits.

The un-named older bi-sexual sculptor Z takes up with in 'long-shabby Hackney Road' (69) educates her both to sexual womanhood and the differences between English and Chinese intimacy (Hanif Kureishi's *Intimacy* becomes one of her most-read books). Soho peep show, contraception and male pub drinking come under her inquiring gaze, as do China's one-child policy, state prudery and poetic vocabulary for intercourse and genitalia. 'Love', articulated from both worlds, will be one of her key entries, as will abortion (she undergoes one in Richmond), and privacy ('privacy makes family fallen apart', 106), separation, age and contradiction. The exhilaration, and also the travail and break-up of first adult relationship, become other entries. The diary accretes from beyond London, to Cornwall, Wales and Dublin, and from encounters of art and other relationship to Z's month-long itinerary through Europe.

'Self' holds an especially pivotal place in the thesaurus. 'We Chinese are not encouraged to use the word "self" so often . . . but here, in this rainy old capitalist country, "self" means everything' (269–70). This play of not quite opposites the Chinese-born but now long London-resident Xiaolu Guo carries off with appealing ingenuity right down to word twists ('Eat afternoon tea?', 'Queue Gardens'). *A Concise Chinese–English Dictionary for Lovers*, amid the novel's wider transnational reference, gives unique astute modern fabling to England and Englishness.

CONTEMPORARY MODERN

Black Britain. Black England. Black London. A thickening folder arises in the literary generations writing since Windrush and the footfalls of postcolonial Africa. In the case of Diran Adebayo's *Some Kind of Black*, as in *Girl, Woman, Other* and *Home Fire*, the focus again allows for any amount of immediacy. North and south of the river, and within them turf boroughs like Tottenham and Camberwell, set locale. Vexed race politics, black in-house as much as black-on-white, hold sway. Street cohorts contend. Local community politicos speak. University and 'first-generation white collar' (93) enter the reckoning. Black PR, tech, media and video career-makers seek their chances and funding. Afro-Englishes, Afro-musics, indie black radio, clubs, raves, hip-hop, weed, sickle-cell anaemia, and African and Caribbean immigrant parental authority and church-going, set the tempo. Young liaisons and courtships, black and black–white 'relationship culture' (56), enter, jar, rise and fade. The story brims with vernacular complexity, as everyday spoken modern as could be wished yet tightly threaded under the novel's impressive hold.

In the figure of Dele the novel also enacts new coming of age. A rare black entrant into Oxford, a graduate in history, he steers uncertainly between what he calls London's 'rasta metaphysics' (15), 'le nubianisme' (190), and the university of 'this postcard town' (27). Home, besides his stentorian Nigerian civil servant father ('One Nation Heathite Tory Man', 44) and pressed clerical worker mother with her Nigerian village memories, means his sister Dapo. Their teasing fondness of relationship is given added intensity by her sickle cell collapses and Middlesex Hospital emergencies. Friendships in the densely peopled round include Concrete, tough school-time blackjack partner, and Gabriel, photographer and sound-recordist of black voices. Lovers, from Oxford to the capital, include the rich fellow-Oxford white girlfriend Helena and the prim black Londoner Cheryl, the no-nonsense black nurse Dawn and the white food-delivery chef Andria. Abeyo writes a busy contemporary modern, the era of black millennials.

The centrepiece, Dele's arrest and beating-up with Concrete and Dapo at the hands of the racist police thug Daniels, together with the unsolved knife-murder at the community protest of the black youth Derek Dalton, puts Dele at the centre of both political and family theatre. Different action groups collide, *Black Fights Back* (BFB) in one stripe, the *Socialist Worker Party* (SWP) in another.

Sol, the moving spirit behind the Yardcore Agency, the PR company Dele joins, turns out to be fiddling the books, an inside trader. The city's black overlaps and fissures, its plays of Jamaican, Bajan and Yoruba-inflected idiom even as Trevor MacDonald and Trevor Phillips speak BBC English, get full recognition. *Some Kind of Black* keeps its narrative pieces up and running.

'He had always been some kind of black' (190) offers the sentence from which the novel's title is taken. Adebayo's debut novel explores the contingency of that identity with full care, modern blackness, modern Englishman, modern Englishness, all bred in the bone and yet still in the making.

The human tree-rings of identity, specifically what it signifies to be a modern Jew and male, not to say a widower, Howard Jacobson's *The Finkler Question* tackles with the same lavish wit at work throughout all his fiction. Comic-modern in mishap yet full of the shadows of ancient history, and seasoned with slivers of argot Yiddish and ritual Hebrew, it theatricalises an infectiously observant round of Anglo-Jewish close encounter. Quite literally so, as it opens with the London mugging within reach of the BBC of one of its three main players, Julian Treslove, himself the non-Jewish would-be Jew, and by a woman no less who in turn may or may not be Jewish. This roundabout proves to be the first of many in the novel, varyingly ethnic, sexual, commemoratory, a Jewish *condition moderne* enacted with the mordant brilliance justly given recognition by the 2010 Booker Prize committee.

The Finkler Question does not 'answer' the Finkler Question, that of what it is or has been to negotiate Jewishness, whether by offence or defence, heedfulness or indifference, and in an England that has been both haven and anti-Semitic. Why should it? Even so, Jacobson shuffles a busy pack but at core a working triangle. Treslove, the lonesome after-hours radio producer, actor-lookalike, has become an aspirant Jew full of self-apprehension, Sam Finkler (full name Samuel Ezra Finkler), Oxford trained media-popular philosopher, has a passion for the Palestinian cause and poker. Libor Sevcik, their Czech-born octogenarian one-time teacher and Hollywood gossip veteran, has operated under the telling showbiz pseudonym of Egon Slick. The friendship that draws them in, close but often brittle, runs alongside their women (Jewish mothers, wives, and *shiksa* converts), a dense modernity of relationship.

CONTEMPORARY MODERN 153

Maimonides and Horovitz. North London and Israel-Palestine. Zionism and the ideological counter-movement under the mutant name of ASHAMED JEWS (abbreviated to ASH). Bedroom and *seder*. Julian's zigzag 'modular' university course and the aesthetics of circumcision and Jewish naming of genitalia. The trio expound their gains and losses within these and kindred matrices. Libor unrestfully mourns his deceased wife Malkie Hofmannsthal. Sam's wife Tyler Gallagher has been felled by cancer before her time. Hephzibah Weizenbaum, Julian's final on-off Jewish amour, or the different mothers of Julian's sons named from Italian opera, Rodolpho and Alfredo ('my sons the goyim', 181), haunt him for all that he has pursued them with passion. Marital and extra-marital fare adds edge, richly seasoned pre- and post-coital dialogue to go along with the actual sex.[6]

'Finkler . . . felt a new book coming on. *The Glass Half Full: Schopenhauer for Teen Binge Drinkers*' (125). So reacts Sam to the uncertain world about him, the 'rationalist and gambler' (224), ready as always with quick-fix philosophy. 'You never know with Jews what was a joke and what wasn't' (148) muses Julian after one of his adulterous love-trysts with Sam's wife Tyler. 'The chicken symbolizes the pleasure Jewish men take in having a team of women cook it for them' (155) observes Libor of the proverbial Jewish menu at one of his soirées. 'Only Jews could be *Jewishly* ashamed' (166) runs an arising comment at an ASHamed meeting held at the Groucho Club. Libor, bereft, tired, commits suicide at his Austro-Hungarian pronounced 'Bitchy 'Ead' (335), grieved over by proto-Jewish Julian in slipped *yarmulke* and would-be un-Jewish Sam Jewishly ever unable to finish saying his *kaddish*.

The whole is brought off within inspired knots of contrariety, Holocaust to *Desert Island Discs*, media careers to sexual desire, and always the glissades of speech and wordplay (pivotally the auditory surreal paradigm of Jew-Judith-June-Juno-Jewno-D'Jew know-Ju, Julian that thinks he hears during the attack). Jacobson's writing absorbs thick tranches of Jewish presence in the world with rare imagination: England, Israel, Anglo-Jewish Museum, anti-Zionist Jews, Marrying Out, Kristallnacht, High Holidays, PLO scarves, the Talmud, Chosen People. His forte lies in keeping the seriousness inside deep preservative wells of humour. Murmurs on occasion have gone up about too immersive a focus, or to borrow a phrase and intonation, more than more than enough already. But the novel takes shape as Jewish *camera lucida* and, like all best comedy, complicated by acts of competition and betrayal, not to say the darker colours of grief. The effect is stirring, both contemporary and modern.

Alan Hollinghurst's *The Line of Beauty*, it became staple observation in the reviews, aims in a number of ways to out-James Henry James, a writer whose name and work recurs in the novel. But as much as the writing has its Jamesian flair, the pirouettes of consciousness and style, Hollinghurst turns James's well-known sublimations about-face. For in the life intervals of Nick Guest, told in the time bands of 1983, 1986 and 1987, the novel moves fluently across high art and low sex, Thatcher triumphalism (tellingly she is referred to as 'Madam') and the looming rise of AIDS. Amid fashionable postcode London, or Le Manoir in rural France, or Lord Kessler's country house Hawkeswood, Hollinghurst renders Nick the symptomatic figure of contemporary modernity in a 1980s England supreme in double standard and spectacle.

Maverick trader greed rubs against old wealth. Private drug and sexual behaviour belies public surface. *Telegraph* and *Sun* editorials assume righteousness even as the politics they canvas, and the finance behind them, mires in corruption. Classic art, the great canons of music, are suborned to new-affluence philistinism. The lavishly catered party, the house musical performance, become covers for private manoeuvre. Hollinghurst does fine business in having his reader witness money talking, political connivance and promotion, sexual hide and seek. Little wonder the novel abounds in tilting mirrors, busy gaze.[7]

New out of Oxford with his First in English, the aesthete, hungrily gay Nick supplies the human fulcrum, at once fey, ironic, yet also sexual opportunist and line of cocaine user.[8] Son of a Northamptonshire antiques dealer, he becomes attic-lodger in the Victorian townhouse of the boorish Tory MP Gerald Fedden and his heiress wife Rachel ('Nick loved the upper-class economy of her talk', 47), he could not better play participant-observer. At the same time he has enrolled at UCL as a PhD candidate working precisely on 'style' in James. The Fedden Silver Wedding party in which Nick dances with Thatcher, who thinks him a 'young don', will in turn be watched feverishly by Gerald and his envying fellow Thatcher-acolytes. The novel compares these theatres of desire with alert and let it be said Jamesian diligence, whether the politics ('all this Toryism and money', 172) or phallic male hunger (Nick is said variously to seek 'aesthetically radiant images of gay activity', 25, and to be 'deliciously brainwashed by sex', 155).

Nick's love affairs, with the black council worker Leo Charles of lower-middle-class 'unknown Willesden' (157), their trysts 'a teeming inward sense of occasion' (35), and with Wani Ourado, son of a newly ennobled House of Lords trader millionaire ('He's Lebanese, he's the only child, he's engaged to be married, his father's a psychopath', 345, and whom Nick 'had sodomized more often than he could remember', 73), co-exist with addiction to the beauty of Chopin, Mozart, classic museum and gallery display, and a modern German luminist painter like Christian Zitt.

Similarly, Nick's long-standing adoration of the athletic Fedden son, Toby, his Oxford contemporary like Wani, bespeaks other beauty for him however much Toby, like his bipolar sister Catherine, belongs to 'the great heterosexual express' (64). Nick could not more en-figure past and present, young arts doyen (his project with Wani's money for a new high-culture magazine and film version of *The Spoils of Poynton*) and Portobello Road and public-toilets cottager. In the company of Ronnie, his supplier, he has grounds to imagine the risk to himself at the prospect of prison for drugs and scandal as 'a pretty little poof with an Oxford accent' (233).

Hollinghurst's prime metaphor, the line of beauty itself, gives thread to the whole in how it derives from William Hogarth's affinity for the ogee or double-curve s-bend in his *Analysis of Beauty* (1753). For Nick, sinuous canvases of the nude or the craft of manicured furniture blend with the 'double curve of (Leo's) lower back' (423) and the copious lines of cocaine. *Ogee* will be the name of the only issue of the magazine planned with Wani. Collapse happens, on the one hand the death of Leo from AIDS and Wani's HIV positive condition, on the other scandal headlines as to Gerald's involvement in asset-stripping fraud and philandering with his aid Penny and allegations of gay orgy in France by Toby and his circle. Nick's expulsion from the Fedden house for supposed betrayal of Gerald acts as both close and opening. Against fracas, the mixed regimes of appetite, the novel uses the ogee curve to greatest advantage as metaphor, an organising reference, for Hollinghurst's dark contemporary fable.

156   MODERNS – CHAUCER TO CONTEMPORARY FICTION

These fictions, in kind with those addressed in prior chapters, inevitably signal the selective arcade. Yet if there is analogy in the different currents of English culture explored in each of the novels, there is equally clear autonomy of imagining, authorial distance far beyond ethnography. It would be inappropriate, a default in attention, to suggest otherwise. Contemporary writers, and so contemporary readerships: yet, and wholly at the same time, both reflect the continuing rhythm of the literary modern.

Notes

1. Three decades ago I endeavoured to take the measure of this diversity. See A. Robert Lee (ed.), *Other Britain, Other British; Contemporary Multicultural Fiction*, London: Pluto Books, 1995.
2. Diran Adebayo, *Some Kind of Black*, London: Virago, 1996. Republished London: Abacus, 1997; Bernardine Evaristo, *Girl, Woman, Other*, Harmondsworth, Middlesex: Penguin Books, 2019, 2020; Xiaolu Guo, *A Concise Chinese–English Dictionary for Lovers*, London: Chatto & Windus, 2007.
3. Kamila Shamsie, *Home Fire*, London: Bloomsbury, 2017; Howard Jacobson, *The Finkler Question*, London: Bloomsbury 2010; Alan Hollinghurst, *The Line of Beauty*, London: Picador.
4. Fyodor Dostoevsky, 'White Nights', originally published separately in 1848, and then in the collection *White Nights and Other Stories*.
5. Hanif Kureishi, *Intimacy*, London: Faber & Faber, 1998, 132.
6. Page references are to the Bloomsbury edition, 2010.
7. In a BBC World Service interview for 4 November 2017, Hollinghurst suggests a parallel between his fiction's version of the 1980s and that of the 1890s in Henry James's fiction, in both the interplays of public and private bad faith.
8. Page references are to the Picador edition, 2004.

Epilogue:
Modern. Modernism.
Postmodernism. Contemporary
Modern

Modern

One goes back to where this account began. Why do certain writings more than others attract the designation of modern? Does being modern have its own history? Can the modern, and moderns, only, or simply, be a matter of seeming new? For certain writers, whether canonical from Chaucer to Conrad, or less so from Skelton to Quin, quite more emphatically than others signal the impulse to make change, challenge the paradigm. That includes the way authorship can be said to work in *The Canterbury Tales*, or the reflexive nature of *Hamlet*, or Donne's poetry when in full throat, or Sterne amid his turns, or novels that refigure 'the modern' from Ford Madox Ford to B. S. Johnson and through to contemporaries like Bernardine Evaristo or Alan Hollinghurst. Theirs is the gallery addressed in the present account, each, it has been my hope to have established, responsible for creating their own kind of invitation. We might keep in mind Oscar Wilde's aphorism in 'The Decay of Lying' (1891): 'It is only the modern that ever becomes old-fashioned'.[1]

Modernism

Modernism, by the third decade of the ongoing century, looks to have more or less arrived at consensus of definition. Agreement approaches as to the vectors in play across national and international

157

158   MODERNS – CHAUCER TO CONTEMPORARY FICTION

literary texts, and to include the visual arts, music, architecture, manifesto, ideology and popular culture. In anglophone literature Eliot, James, Joyce or Woolf usually head the column. But they have had company. A focus on women's modern, other than Woolf, offers too easily sidelined cases in point. The imagism of Mina Loy, the serialism of Dorothy Richardson or the fusion into postcolonialism of Jean Rhys refer their modern turn towards the more inclusive range of modernism. The sightings on offer are aimed at this fuller grasp, the wider sighting. In his study of Robert Louis Stevenson, Alan Sandison poses the relevant question: 'So far as I know there isn't an essay called '*when* was modernism?'.[2]

Postmodern

The concept of the postmodern, the proposition that truth relies equally on the truth-teller and ownership of telling, has stirred its fair degree of controversy in literature as elsewhere. Jean-François Lyotard's contention that grand narratives deceive, and that writing the world better proceeds as *petits récits*, early made its appeal. Counter-voices said no: there indeed are truths, realities, which literature must still hold to and proclaim. An allied term like meta-modernism gives hints of the post-postmodern. In B. S. Johnson and Ann Quin postmodern English fiction, and conceivably its aftermath, found avatars, their novels would-be heirship to Joyce or to the New Novel. In this regard they might duly be thought signallers of modernism's literary twilight, authors with their own subsequent purchase on the text 'where everything is possible'. Vaclav Havel in his *Liberty Medal Speech* delivered in Philadelphia in 1994 supplies the historically more contextual gloss: 'We live in the postmodern world, where everything is possible and almost nothing is certain'.[3]

Contemporary Modern

Historicisation does its work, the given fiction, poem or drama fitted into time-scheme or shelved into sequences of decade. The process takes on added layering, new twist, in the context of contemporary technology, the media age variously of ebook or hypertext, Ipad or Iphone, headphone or open access. Trigger warnings add to the shape-shifts. Literature successively thought modern, or even the one or another contemporary version of the modern, itself in turn

EPILOGUE 159

so becomes newly modernised. The authors at hand in *Moderns – Chaucer to Contemporary Fiction* take literary imagining beyond simply the new, or even simply the avant-garde, but rather into a diverse contemporary 'modern' dispensation with its own equally diverse operating terms of idiom. It would not be out of order to cite W. H. Auden:

At first critics classified authors as Ancients, that is to say, Greek and Latin authors, and Moderns, that is to say every post-Classical Author. Then they classified them by eras, the Augustans, the Victorians, etc., and now they classify them by decades, the writers of the '30', '40's. etc. Very soon, it seems they will be labelling authors, like automobiles, by the year.

Notes

1. Oscar Wilde, 'The Decay of Lying: An Observation. A Dialogue', 1891. *Complete Works of Oscar Wilde*, London and Glasgow: Collins, 1948, 970–92.
2. Alan Sandison, *Robert Louis Stevenson and the Appearance of Modernism: A Future Feeling*, London: Faber & Faber, 1996, 12.
3. Vaclav Havel, *Liberty Medal Speech*, Philadelphia, 1994.

Index

Abse, Danny, 'Talking to Myself',
    36
Adebayo, Diran, 8, 145, 151–2
    Some Kind of Black, 145,
    151–2
Ali, Monica, 145
Alvarez, A, 53
Amis, Kingsley, 135
Amis, Martin, 135, 145
Aristotle, 63
Arnold, Matthew, 84, 95
Assis, Machado de, *Dom*
    Casmurro, 64
Auden, W. H., 158
Auerbach, Erich, *Mimesis: The*
    Presentation of Reality in
    Western Literature, 40
Austen, Jane, 6, 78
    Sense and Sensibility, 6

Bacon, Francis, 40
Bailey, Paul, 145
Balzac, Honoré de, 63
Barnes, Julian, 36, 37, 145
    Flaubert's Parrot, 36
Barthes, Roland, 69
Beckett, Samuel, 45, 64, 134, 136
    Malloy, 64
    The Unnameable, 136
Beckford, William, 74
Berengarten, Richard, 39
    A Portrait in Interviews, 39
Blake, William, 6
Bloom, Harold, 41

Boccaccio, 17
Boethius, *Consolations of*
    Philosophy, 10
Borges, Jorge Luis, *Ficciones*, 64
Boswell, James, 63
Bourdin, Martial, 108
Bradbury, Malcolm, 135
Braine, John, 135
Branagh, Kenneth, 41
Brontë, Charlotte, 8
    Jane Eyre, 8, 129–30
Brontës, The, 78
Brookner, Anita, 145
Brook-Rose, Christine, *Such*,
    134
Brooks, Cleanth, *The Well*
    Wrought Urn, 53
Brophy, Bridgid, *In Transit: An*
    Heroi–Cyclic Novel, 134
Burbage, Richard, 41
Burke, Edmund, 85
Burns, Alan, *After the Rain*, 134
Butler, Samuel, 3, 7, 95, 97–9, 106
    Erewhon, 95
    Notebooks, 95
    The Way of All Flesh, 7, 95,
    97–9
Butler, Samuel, *Hudibras*, 81
Byatt, A. S., 145
Byron, Lord, 6, 73, 74–7;
    Childe Harold, 6–7, 73, 75–7
    Don Juan, 6–7, 40, 73, 75, 82,
    English Bards and Scotch
    Reviewers, 74

INDEX

'Beppo: A Venetian Stry', 74
'Cain', 74
'Manfred', 74
'The Vision of Judgment', 74

Chaucer, Geoffrey, 1, 3–4, 4–5,
10–25,157
Boece, 10
Book of Troilus, 10
Parlement of Foules, 35
The Book of the Duchess, 10
Tale of Caunterbury, 10
The Canterbury Tales, 5, 11,
17, 24
The House of Fame, 10
'General Prologue', 17–20
'Lenvoy de Chaucer', 17, 20,
24
'The Franklin's Tale', 21
'The Knight's Tale', 22
'The Man of Law's Tale', 23
'The Merchant's Tale', 21
'The Miller's Tale', 20–1, 22
'The Nun's Priests Tale', 23
'The Prioress's Tale', 11
'The Physician's Tale', 23
'The Tale of Melabee', 5, 11,
15–16, 23
'Tale of Thopas', 5, 11–15, 17,
21, 23
'The Wife of Bath's Tale', 21
Camus, Albert, 45
Carew, Thomas, 'Elegie upon the
Death of the Deane of Paul's,
Dr. John Donne', 52
Carter, Angela, 145
Cervantes, Miguel de, 63, 74
Cicero, 31, 63
Cobbett, William
Political Register, 84
Rural Rides, 84
Coleridge, Samuel Taylor, 25, 73,
81–2, 86
Biographia Literaria, 81–2

Collins, William, 74
Conrad, Joseph, 3, 7–8, 103,
107–22, 157
Nostromo, 108
The Secret Agent, 7–8, 107–22
Under Western Eyes, 36
Conrad, Joseph, and Ford, Ford
Madox, 103
Romance, 103
The Inheritors, 103
Cooper, Thomas, 74
Cortázar, Julio, *Rayuela,* 136
Cowley, Abraham, 54; *The
Mistress,* 54
Crashaw, Richard, 'A Hymn to
Sainte Teresa', 54

Dante, 55, 74
Degas, Edgar, 103
DeLillo, Don, *White Noise,*
65
De Quincy, Thomas, 52
Dickens, Charles, 95,
Dickstein, Morris, 'An Outsider
in his Own Life' (review),
40
Diogenes, 31
Donne, John, 6, 52–62, 53, 157
'A Holy *Sonnet*', 60
'A Litanie' 60
'A Valediction: of the Booke',
6, 53, 55–6
'A Valediction: Of Weeping',
53
'Divine Reflections, Sonnet
XIV', 55, 60
'Good Friday, 1613, Rising
Westward', 60
'The Canonization', 53, 57
'The good tomorrow', 58
'The Sunne Rising', 57
'The Triple Fool', 56
'The Will, 59
'To Mr. S.B.', 55

162 MODERNS – CHAUCER TO CONTEMPORARY FICTION

Dostoevsky, Fyodor, 109
  Crime and Punishment, 109
  Notes from Underground, 109
  The Devils, 109
  The Idiot, 109
  The Possessed, 109
  'White Nights', 146
Dryden, John, 52, 63
Duchamp, Marcel, 125
Duncan, Isadora, 124

Eel, Roberta, 68
Eliot, George, 73, 78, 95
  Adam Bede, 73
Eliot, T. S., 3, 6, 41, 52–3, 54,
  135, 158
  'The Love Song of J. Alfred
    Prufrock', 52, 126
  'The Metaphysical Poets' 53
  'The Waste Land', 52, 55, 103
Emecheta, Buchi, 145
Empson, William, *Seven Types of
  Ambiguity*, 53
Erasmus, 63
Evaristo, Bernardine, 4, 8,145,
  146–8, 152
  Girl, Woman, Other, 4, 145,
  146–8, 152

Faulkner, William, *The Sound and
  the Fury*, 114
Feinstein, Elaine, 145
Figes, Eva, *Light*, 134–5
Fish, Stanley, 69
Flaubert, Gustave, 36, 103
  'Un Coeur Simple', 36
Ford, Ford Madox, 3, 7, 95, 96,
  103–5, 106
  No More Parades, 103
  The Good Soldier, 7, 95, 103–5
Forster, E. M., 35, 67–8, 99
Fraser, G. F., 2, 3
  *The Modern Writer and His
    World*, 2

Gardner, Helen, 53
Garrick, David, 41
Godwin, William, 81, 86
Goethe, Johann Wolfgang, *The
  Sorrows of Young Werther*,
  81
Gogol, Nikolai, 45, 63
Golding, William, 135
Goldsmith, Oliver, 63, 74
Gordon, Ian Alistair, 27
Goya, Francisco, 45
Goytisolo, Juan, *Count Julian*, 64
Graham, Cunningham, 108
Graves, Robert, 26, 36
  Oxford Addresses on Poetry,
  26
Gray, Thomas, 74
Grierson, H. T. C., 6, 52
  Donne's Poetical Works, 52,
  (ed.) *Metaphysical Lyrics and
    Poems of the Seventeenth
    Century: Donne to Butler*,
  52–3
Griffiths, Jane, *John Skelton and
  Poetic Authority; Defining the
  Liberty to Speak*, 32
Guo, Xiaolu, 8, 146, 149–50
  *A Concise Chinese-English
    Dictionary for Lovers*, 146,
  149–50
Gurnah, Abdulrazak, 145

Hardy, Thomas, 35
Havel, Vaclav, 158
Hazlitt, William, 3, 7, 40, 47,
  84–94
  *Characters of Shakespear's
    Plays*, 7, 84, 89–90
  Lectures on the English Poets,
  7, 84, 89
  Liber Amoris, 85
  Life of Napoleon, 85
  Political Essays, 84, 85
  The Plain Speaker, 84

INDEX 163

Table Talk, 7, 84
The Spirit of the Age, 7, 84, 85
'A Farewell to Essay-Writing',
  87–8
'Montaigne', 93
'Mr. Coleridge', 88–9
'Mr. Wordsworth', 88
'My First Acquaintance with the
  Poets', 86–7
'On a Sun-Dial, 92
'On Familiar Style', 86
'On Shakespeare and Milton',
  89
'On the Pleasure of Painting', 87
'The Fight', 7, 91
'The Indian Jugglers', 7, 91–2
'The Lake School', 88
Hemingway, Ernest, 103
Heppenstall, Reynar, *The
  Connecting Door,* 134
Herbert, George, 'The Collar', 54,
Hoffer, Eric, *Truth Imagined,* 40
Hogarth, William, 65
Hollinghurst, Alan 8, 146, 154–5
  The Line of Beauty, 146, 154–5
Holroyd, Michael, 96
Hopkins, Gerard Manley, 29
Horace, 63
Hughes, Ted, 35
Hume, David, 86
Huxley, Aldous, *Chrome Yellow,*
  82

Iser, Wolfgang, 69
Ishiguro, Kazuo, 145

Jacobson, Howard, 8, 146, 152–4
  The Finkler Question, 146,
  152–4
James, Henry, 3, 103
  The Princess Casamassima, 103
Johnson, B. S., 1, 4, 8, 134, 135–40,
  158
  Albert Angelo, 136, 137

*Aren't You Rather Too Young
  to be Writing Your Memoirs?,*
  136
Fat Man on a Beach, 135
*House Mother Normal: A
  Geriatric Comedy,* 8, 138–40
*See the Old Lady Decently
  Buried,* 135
The Unfortunates, 8, 64–5, 134,
  135, 136–8, 143
Travelling People, 135, 137
*You're Human Like the Rest of
  Them,* 135
Johnson, Dr Samuel, 6, 52,63, 85
  *Preface to the Plays of William
  Shakespeare,* 89
  'Cowley', 6, 41
Jonson, Ben, 52
Joyce, James, 3, 64, 67, 123, 134,
  135, 136, 158
  Ulysses, 103
Juvenal, 31

Kafka, Franz, 45
Karloff, Boris, 78
Keats, John, 35, 56, 73, 85
Kerouac Jack, 39
  Desolation Angels, 39
  On the Road, 143
Kermode, Frank, 1, 2, 3
  Continuities, 1_
Keyes, Sydney, 'The Parrot', 36
Kierkegaard, S ren, 45
Klee, Paul, 6
Kundera, Mlilan, 63
Kureishi, Hanif, 145, 146
  Intimacy, 146
Kyd, Thomas, *The Spanish
  Tragedy,* 41

Laforgue, Jules, 54
Lamb, Charles, 84, 85
Lamb, Charles and Mary, 86
Lamming, George, 145

164 MODERNS – CHAUCER TO CONTEMPORARY FICTION

Lawrence, D. H., 64
Leavis, F. R., 53, 63
  'The Line of Wit', 53
Lee, Christopher, 78
Leishman, J. B., 53
Lewis, C. S., 26, 27
Lewis, Wyndham, 103
Locke, John, 63, 85
  Essay on Human
    Understanding, 63
Lodge, David, 135
Longinus, 63
Loy, Mina, 3, 8, 124–7, 132, 158
  Insel, 125
  Lunar Baedeker, 124, 125–7
  Stories and Essays, 125
  'Feminist Manifesto', 125
  'Lunar Baedeker', 127
  'Parturition', 26
  'Songs to Joannes', 125–6
Lugosi, Bela, 78
Lyotard, Jean-François, 158

McEwan, Ian, 39, 49, 145
  Nutshell, 49
  Saturday, 39
Marvell, Andrew, 'To His Coy
  Mistress', 54
Matthiessen, F. O., 53
Maupassant, Guy de, 103
Maurier, Daphne du, *Rebecca*, 78
Melville, Herman, *The Confidence
  Man*, 82
Menippus, 63
Middleton, Thomas, Tourneur,
  Cyril, *The Revenger's
  Tragedy*, 41
Milton, John, 74, 79
  Paradise Lost, 79
Monet, Claude, 103, 134
Montaigne, Michel de, 40, 63
  'Apologie de Raymond Sebond',
    40
  'Que sais-je'? 40

Morrison, Toni, *Beloved*,
  78
Murdoch, Iris, 49, 135
  The Black Prince, 49

Nietzsche, Friedrich, 40

Okri, Ben, 145
Olivier, Laurence, 41
Orwell, George, 84
Ovid, 17, 31

Paulin, Tom, *The Day-Star of
  Liberty: William Hazlitt's
  Radical Style*, 84
Peacock, Thomas Love, 6, 7, 73,
  80–2
  Crotchet Castle, 80, 82
  Gryll Grange, 80
  Headlong Hall, 80
  Nightmare Abbey, 7, 73,
    80–2
Petrarch, 17, 31, 55, 74
  'Laura', 55
Pindar, 55
Pinter, Harold, 134
Plato, 19
Plutarch, 31
Poe, Edgar Allen, 35, 78
  *The Narrative of Arthur
    Gordon Pym*, 78
Pope, Alexander, 52
Pritchett, V. S., 96
Pound, Ezra, 2, 103, 124
  Make It New, 2

Quin, Ann, 1, 4, 8, 123, 134, 135;
  140–3, 157, 158
  Berg, 8, 134
  Passages, 140
  *The Unmapped Country: Stories
    & Fragments*, 143
  Three, 8, 140, 142–3
  Tripticks, 140

INDEX

Radcliffe, Ann, 74, 81
   Udolpho, 81
Rabelais, François, 63
Ray, Man, 125
Rembrandt, 84
Renoir, Pierre-Auguste, 103
Richardson, Dorothy, 3, 8, 124,
   127–9, 132, 158
   Backwater, 127
   Clear Horizon, 127
   Deadlock, 127
   Interim, 127
   Painted Roofs, 124, 127,
     128–9
   Left Hand, 127
   March Moonlight, 127
   Oberland, 127
   Revolving Lights, 127
   The Honeycombe, 127
   The Trap, 127
   The Tunnel, 127
Rimbaud, Arthur, 54
Rhys, Jean, 3, 8, 103, 124, 129–31,
   132, 158
   After Leaving Mr. MacKenzie,
     129
   Good Morning, Midnight, 129
   Quartet, 129
   *Smile Please: An Unfinished
     Autobiography*, 129
   *The Left Bank and Other
     Stories*, 8
   Tigers Are Better Looking,
     129
   Voyage in the Dark, 129
   Wide Sargasso Sea, 8, 124,
     129–31
Robbe-Grillet, Alain, 134
Roffey, Monique, 145
Rousseau, Jean-Jacques, 74,
   85
Rubens, Bernice, 145
Rushdie, Salman, 63–4, 145
   Midnight's Children, 63–4

Sackville-West, Vita, 123
Sainte-Beuve, Charles-Augustin,
   40
Saintsbury, George, 63
Saporta, Marc, *The Quest*, 136
Sexton, Anne, 123
Shakespeare, William, 3, 4, 39–51,
   74
   Hamlet, 3, 5–6, 39–51, 157
Shamsie, Kamila, 8, 145, 148–9,
   152
   Home Fire, 145, 148–9, 152
Shelley, Percy Bysshe, 35, 73, 81
Shelley, Mary Wolstonecraft, 4, 6,
   7, 73, 78–80, 82
   *Frankenstein; or, The New
     Prometheus*, 4, 7, 73, 78–80
Shiraishi, Kazuko, 'Parrot', 36, 37
Sillitoe, Alan, 135
Sinclair, Clive, 145
Skelton, John, 5, 26–38, 147
   'Colyn Clout', 5, 26, 27
   'Phyllyp Sparrow', 5, 26, 27
   'Speke Parrot', 5, 26, 29, 32–5,
     36
   The Bouge of Court', 26, 29–30
   'The Garland of Laurel', 26, 31
   'Why Come Ye Not to Court?',
     5, 26, 30–1
Smith, Zadie, 145
Southey, Robert, 74, 89
Spectator Magazine, 7
Spenser, Edmund, 55
Stein, Gertrude, 124
Sterne, Laurence, 3, 6, 63–73
   *A Sentimental Journey Through
     France and Italy*, 63
   Tristram Shandy, 6, 63–73, 136
Stevens Wallace, 1, 35
   Opus Posthumous, 1–2
Stevenson, Robert Louis, 78, 84,
   158
   *The Strange Case of Dr. Jekyll
     and Mr. Hyde*, 78

166   MODERNS – CHAUCER TO CONTEMPORARY FICTION

Stoker, Bram, *Dracula*, 78
Stoppard, Tom, *Rosencrantz and Guildenstern Are Dead*, 49
Strachey, Lytton, 3, 7, 95–6, 97, 99–103, 106
   Eminent Victorians, 7, 95, 99–103
   Queen Victoria, 96
Swift, Jonathan, 83
   A Tale of a Tub, 63
Sydney, Sir Philip, 55

Theroux, Alexander, *Darconville's Cat*, 64
Titian, 84
transatlantic review, 103
Turgenev, Ivan, *Virgin Soil*, 103
Tuve, Rosamund, 53

Valéry, Paul, 54
Van Vechten, Carl, 124
Verlaine, Paul, 54
Voltaire, 74

Wain, John, 135
Walpole, Horace, *Otranto*, 81

Wanning, Andrews, 53
Waters, Sarah, 145
Wells, H. G., 103
Wilde, Oscar,
   De Profundis, 41
   'The Decay of Lying', 157
Williams, William Carlos, 103
Winterson, Jeannette, 145
Wollstonecraft, Mary, 81
Woolf, Virginia, 3, 8, 63, 64, 84, 123, 158
   A Room of One's Own, 123, 124
   Between the Acts, 124
   Mrs. Dalloway, 124
   The Waves, 124
   Three Guineas, 124
   To the Lighthouse, 124
Wordsworth, William, 7, 88
   The Excursion, 88
   The Lyrical Ballads, 6, 88
Wu, Duncan, *William Hazlitt: The First Modern Man*, 84

Yeats, W. B., 35

Zola, Emile, 109

www.ingramcontent.com/pod-product-compliance
Lightning Source LLC
LaVergne TN
LVHW050047200525
811683LV00004B/49